IN SIGHT

A PSYCHIATRIST'S MEMOIR EXPLORING THE JUNGLE OF THE UNCONSCIOUS

DOLORES FURTCH

To my daughter, an extraordinary human being

To my patients, thanks for allowing me to accompany you thru the roughest times

To all children that unknowingly carry the weight of their parents' stories

CONTENTS

CHAPTER 1

IN THE JUNGLE

IN THE UNCONSCIOUS, *nothing is ever forgotten.*
  -paraphr. Freud

I searched for a seat, but all I saw were potato sacks.

"You can sit on top of onions or potatoes. You choose," said the pilot, waving his hand toward the sacks.

I was headed to Tres Esquinas, a military base along the Orteguaza River, surrounded by piranha-infested water, jungle, and the threat of guerrilla soldiers. In Colombia, once you finish medical school, you must do one year of social service. I chose to complete my year of service at Tres Esquinas, disregarding how dangerous I knew it would be. Natives lived in the jungles around the base and, always suspicious of the military, could be violent and unpredictable. It was chaotic, fast-paced work. I had a few other options for where to go, but none of the calm and boring options sounded good. I was impulsive back then, barely in my twenties, jumping into all my decisions, and feeling damn invincible while also terrified. It made no sense, but it's who I was.

As a new doctor, I didn't know what to expect when I headed to this base. The pilot barely spoke to me and expected me to sit on a sack of potatoes for the ride. I was irritated, but I didn't argue. I knew that Tres Esquinas was a small base, and comfort and safety wouldn't be part of the job. The base only had two planes: a huge one from World War II, which supplied food for the whole base, and a tiny plane with only two seats. I was riding on the grocery plane.

I settled onto the lumpy bag, and we took off. *Ay, Dios Mio.* Oh, my God.

What a thing—flying—even from a sack of potatoes. I've always loved watching planes fly overhead, so being in a plane was a thrill. At the time, I thought the thrill was the attraction to planes.

Looking back, I understand there was more to it than that. My baby brother's gravesite is near a model airplane field, and when I was little, I'd sit there with him, telling him about our broken family and flailing my arms, trying to catch the tiny planes as they disappeared into the sky. Somewhere deep in my unconscious mind, being in a plane meant being far, far away from our family, out of their reach, like my baby brother was.

The pilot announced we'd be landing soon, and I peered out the window to catch my first glimpse of the place I would call home. You could barely even see it from above, blocked as it was by the thick vegetation. The entire compound was just a few white houses huddled together like a tiny neighborhood, with a hangar that housed the administrative offices and, of course, the planes and military equipment. It seemed normal, despite being a handful of structures surrounded by wilderness.

Later it became clear that Tres Esquinas wasn't a large, key military base where the military sent its best and most competent officers. It was where the Air Force sent its troublemakers—a kind of exile for pilots who had stepped out of line. A punishment post. But even if someone had told me beforehand, I don't think it would've mattered. I was young, chasing experience, and full of fight. Rowdy men didn't scare me. After what I was used to from my own scary father, no young man could. A jungle base full of reckless men sounded like where I belonged, right where I fit.

I would end up married to one of the pilots before I knew any better. *Qué suerte.* How lucky.

The potatoes below me shifted as our plane bumped onto the tarmac, knocking me off balance. I regained my footing and took a deep breath, straightening my t-shirt and bracing for my new life.

"Here's your bike." The pilot chuckled as he handed me my bike, the same one I'd been riding since I was eight years old.

I shifted my bag on my back, snatched my bike, and headed off the plane.

Once we got off the plane, we were greeted by a line of olive-skinned officers, all pilots. One of them, a thin, flat-faced young man with an expression that was somewhere between playful and devious, came toward me. His name tag, which was halfway off his uniform, said Emilio.

"Hola."

"Give me this," he said as he rubbed his hand across my watch.

I didn't understand why I needed to take off my watch, but I did it. He sauntered back to the line of soldiers, leaving me confused and annoyed. In my head, I decided to call him *cara'e plato*, flat like a dinner plate.

The rest of us—another doctor, myself, and a nurse—stood opposite them. They called us *rurales,* or doctors who were on their year's service outside of the city. We waited for someone to tell us where to go or what came next. Across the way, a few soldiers nudged each other and wagged their eyebrows like dumbass schoolboys. The pool next to us filled the air with the smell of chlorine and something rotten. I wrinkled my nose, unsure why a pool was even there, much less why it looked like it hadn't been cleaned in years. Gross.

While I stared at the water in disgust, the soldiers suddenly rushed toward us. I knew what was going to happen, and there was no way I could prevent it. One of them, without warning, swept me up and threw me over his shoulder like I weighed nothing. I screamed and punched his back, demanding that he put me down.

Then, I hit the water.

Fuck no. It was cold, full of slime and god-knows-what-else, and disgusting. Turns out, that was part of their stupid initiation ritual, everyone gets tossed into the pool on their first day. As the compound's new *rurales,* I would not recommend the practice from a health perspective. Or a common-sense perspective. I surfaced sputtering. *Qué ridiculez.* What a ridiculous thing. It took days to get the stench of the water out of my hair.

Emilio returned my watch. At the time, I appreciated the gesture, though years later Emilio admitted that he came up to me that day, not because he wanted to preserve my watch as a favor but because he thought it looked cheap and wouldn't survive the pool. To Emilio, anything that didn't shine and glitter meant "cheap." Still, I didn't have to replace my watch. I was not used to men looking out for me, even if the real reason had been more insulting than thoughtful.

There was a small town near the base called Mandalay, the same as my childhood neighborhood. The town had a sorcerer who was known as "the toothless." She might have been in her forties but hadn't aged well. Her clothes were always disheveled on her little body. She cooked and did laundry for the officers. Everybody knew she did black magic with our underwear. Sometimes, she talked to me about *brujería*, witchcraft, how she used it to heal soldiers, and how she used it to put hexes on her enemies. I was always nice to her, though, mainly because she scared the crap out of me.

I went to her house once. The place smelled like she smoked a hundred cigarettes a day. As we sat talking, she took out a photo album.

"There, choose your husband," she said as she tossed me the album.

I flipped open the book, and there were photos of every soldier on base. I don't know why she had all these photos. I shrugged and started flipping through the book. As I turned the pages, I was amused by this odd catalog of men in uniform. I stopped when I saw Emilio.

"Oh, it's him," I said, pointing at his picture. Before that moment, I didn't have any expectation that I would marry *cara'e plato*; finding a man had been the furthest thing from my mind. But I recognized him from that first day and remembered about the watch. She just nodded.

Shortly after, I started talking to Emilio more and more, and it led on naturally from there. We became friendly and started dating. I didn't feel passion for him; I wouldn't have recognized it if I had. But I felt safe and companionable with him, and that was novel in and of itself. He liked to venture out from the base, and I liked to spend my time with him. The Colombian Amazon is magic and enigmatic. Its chaos and uncertainty felt right to me, like home, and I felt confident I could be in full control. I was wrong.

In the jungle, I picked up new ways to care for patients, and I worked each day in the hospital, handling everyday accidents and illnesses. Most days, the work was manageable—treating feet for jungle rot, solving dehydration, bandaging infected cuts, curing the occasional abdominal pain, and delivering babies. A lot of my patients were kids with fevers or scrapes from roughhousing in the heat, or elders complaining of chest pain that turned out to be gas. It was the kind of steady, everyday medicine that gave structure to the chaos of life in the jungle.

Sometimes, Aboriginal groups would travel by river for hours to see me. They spoke no Spanish, so we could only communicate rudimentarily. They brought pineapples and porcupines as trade for the simple medical treatment we gave.

One day, two young Indigenous siblings—a boy and a girl, maybe six and four—were rushed into the emergency room. From what little we could understand from the natives, we gathered that they'd been out on a school trip down the river when someone realized they were ill. They quickly became unconscious, their small bodies limp, foam bubbling from their mouths.

We did everything we knew to do—we started compressions, intubated, pumped meds into their veins, everything by the book. The boy and girl were both in cardiac arrest. We worked on them until we couldn't anymore.

I was the one who had to tell their father. I arranged for their bodies to be transferred to the morgue the next day.

About six hours later, I had dinner in silence and collapsed into bed, drained.

Then, somehow—hours later—the boy woke up.

The staff whispered about jungle *brujería*. I didn't particularly believe in resurrection stories, not even the original one. But it seemed for anything that the boy simply came back to life. The girl, sadly, did not.

At that time, I was puzzled. I thought about toxins as a possible cause, but we did not have a definitive diagnosis. Years later, I read about curare, and I thought about the children. Curare is a paralyzing poison derived from a jungle plant, and it's been used for hunting. Perhaps if I had thought about this plant and understood its effects, I could have saved them, but of course the rural hospital did not have the antidote either. That level of control was not in my reach and never would be.

In the jungle, I lived with three other grads—a doctor, a dentist, and a nurse—in what everyone on base called the "witches' house." The place was covered in cockroaches; they came out of the walls. I hated hearing them scurry around at night. There were bats flapping all over the place outside, threatening to come into the house. Tarantulas crawled out of the drainpipes. We were all young and fresh out of school. We had little privacy. We were all quiet and a bit timid, still learning how to be young professionals.

I started med school at sixteen and graduated as a valedictorian at twenty-one. I was laser-focused—very few parties, no movies, no distractions. Just books, anatomy charts, and sleepless nights with stomach cramps from stress and shitty eating habits. I didn't see it then, but my obsession with my studies and desperation to be perfect was less about medicine and more about survival. Med school wasn't just a career path—it was my escape plan from my chaotic homelife.

My family has always been a clusterfuck. They carry generations of trauma in their minds and on their backs. They ran from violence the way others run from the rain. That violence didn't stay outside—it bled into our living room, our dinner table, our family road trips. Fights, danger, and silence lingered. There was no time for anything soft or emotional. I threw everything I had into school because that —and only that—was what I could control. I figured if I studied hard enough, I could get out for good.

School came with its own kind of violence. Professors groped me, trapped me against lockers, and kissed me against my will. I fought back, cursing and threatening them, but they didn't care.

I reported it. Nothing happened.

I did clinical rotations in some of the city's most dangerous hospitals. I worked in a morgue so packed with corpses that you had to pick what kind of death you wanted to learn from that day—gunshots, tumors, pregnancies gone wrong. There were flies everywhere. I kept Vicks VapoRub under my nose to try to hide the god-awful stench. We didn't have gowns to wear, just cheap black garbage bags.

During my clinical rotation in the psychiatric ward, I finally felt like I found my place. It sounds insane that psychotic people made me feel calm, but it did. The doctors there didn't hide behind stiff coats and egos—they wore corduroy pants and talked about art, literature, and humanities like it was part of daily life, ideas I had never heard echoes of. I learned more about the unconscious mind in that rotation than I did in years of lectures.

The unconscious is silent—under our awareness—and yet it spills into everything we do. Our decisions, who we are, where we feel like we belong—it all springs from that dark well that we cannot ever be fully aware of.

All the while, I could see this mental suffering in others, but I could not see any of my own. My body knew better, and frequent stomach and chest pains landed me in the emergency room often. Tests showed nothing but gastritis from a poor diet, but I demanded to see specialists. Once, a doctor suggested I see a psychologist, and I was deeply offended.

If something was wrong with me, it was in my body, not my mind, I was foolishly certain.

Moving to the house in the jungle was not my end goal, but it was a step. I was making a new life for myself outside of my family. Leave the past behind. Shut the chest for good.

What I failed to understand then, what would take me *years* of experiencing life to realize, is that I was foolish to think I could leave the past behind. You carry it all with you, in that dark well of the unconscious.

The other women on the base were like me; we didn't party much—we were too busy, too tired, or just too disinterested in whatever mess the men had planned. We always showed up for the new pilot celebrations though. After their first solo flights, the tradition for the pilot was to get absolutely wasted on cheap liquor, the kind better suited for cleaning than drinking. Not a toast or a congratulations speech but forced binge drinking: shots lined up, beers chugged, all cheered on until the poor guy couldn't stand straight.

It was so gross when they'd throw up. It would just pour out of their noses and mouths. They wouldn't even clean it up either. It wasn't how I would've wanted to be celebrated, and it didn't look fun. Plus, it didn't stop there. After the liquor came the beatdown—senior pilots would chase the newbie around with long planks of wood, smacking him while everyone laughed. Occasionally they would release an angry dog named Pipo to bite the pilot. Pipo never disappointed. Then they'd soak the pilot in plane oil as if he were being baptized, and chuck him into the muddy, piranha-filled river. Just another one of the senseless ways they amused themselves.

Watching the pilots interact was like watching a pack of overgrown boys at recess. They teased, tackled, wrestled, and roughhoused constantly, always on the verge of starting a full-blown fight. It was testosterone and immaturity turned all the way up. But somehow, it didn't matter. I was in my element: the buzz of planes overhead and the unpredictable energy.

I never thought about the danger. The base was surrounded by guerrilla groups. I just enjoyed feeling alive, free from all the responsibilities of the clusterfuck back home.

When I wasn't working, I was with Emilio. He was funny as hell, telling the dumbest jokes with barely a punchline. He would bring me lunch at the hospital sometimes—it was a nice break from working. He talked about his life constantly. I barely knew the guy, but I knew his family tree and all the names of his dogs back home; he said whatever came to his mind. I wasn't used to a man being so chatty.

My father didn't play around or ever talk friendly with us. He would just beat my mom and sister, then he would leave, then come back and repeat. I threatened to stab him once, so he would leave my mom in peace. That was probably why he didn't hurt me the way he hurt them. I would fight back and mean it.

Emilio, on the other hand, was harmless and light-hearted. He made the base feel less like prison and more like summer camp—dangerous, yes, but fun.

Emilio took me to hideouts around the base that I was pretty sure I wasn't supposed to know about—abandoned towers, tree-covered trails, busted-out bunkers. I'd hesitate, nervous about getting in trouble, and he'd tell me it would be okay. He would typically minimize the seriousness of any situation. I hated being told what to do, but I wasn't going to back down from a challenge either, so I'd follow him.

In hindsight, Emilio was not the best example of what an officer should look like. His heart was in the right place, sometimes, but his mind wandered or was barely there. When walking at night or in the dense jungle where you couldn't be seen at all, a soldier standing watch would ask for the password of the day. Their orders were to shoot if we did not know the password. Emilio never knew the password. We would just laugh and scream back, "We don't know it." They never shot at us.

Emilio treated his job like a joke most of the time. When he was "officer of the day," he was supposed to patrol the base for twenty-four hours on a bike, but he mostly napped through it, snoring loudly and carelessly. I called him out once, and he shrugged: "Nothing's gonna happen. And if it does? There's nothing we can do about it anyway." This was classic Emilio. Careless, unbothered, and deeply unserious.

Of course, later I would look back on these days and see so many signs of what we now know as Attention Deficit Hyperactive Disorder (ADHD). Emilio was distracted, restless, and easily bored. He had problems planning and completing tasks. In that jungle, I was careless and irresponsible, and I knew it. But the jungle, to me, was a much-needed respite from everything I'd known before—tarantulas, chaos, and dangers in the dark be damned.

And Emilio, in all his careless antics, was so different from other men I'd known. I wasn't a pilot, but through Emilio I still got to know the life of a pilot. He shared his flying stories with me, laughing off his learning mistakes as though he wasn't flying a tiny bus hundreds of miles in the air, because he loved it and that's who he was—a pilot.

I was flying, too, overwhelmed by the thrill and novelty of the jungle. Time with Emilio felt like I was moving toward my little brother, long lost in the sky with the planes.

I never stopped to consider what would happen to a pilot if he were to lose his plane.

CHAPTER 2

TICKET OUT

EMILIO and I found out we were pregnant after a year of dating. It was a shock, because I had been taking oral contraceptives. The pregnancy was further proof of how little control I had, which made me feel sick all the time. What if the baby turned out deformed from the medication? How would I continue my specialty training? In Colombia, the stigma against premarital pregnancy was real.

We decided he would need to leave the Air Force. We couldn't raise a baby in the jungle. When he quit, we moved back to Bogotá, where Emilio planned to fly commercial planes. Emilio was raised in Bogotá and felt confident applying to all the big airlines there. To become a commercial pilot, he had to take a series of psychological tests, which he failed to pass. He never knew why, but it had to be because of his ADHD. (It would be about ten years into our marriage before I gave him this diagnosis.)

When I asked him about the psychological tests, he minimized the issue and claimed that none of the airlines had open positions so they couldn't bring him in. His father, a well-known cardiologist in the city, even tried to use his influence to advocate for Emilio with the airlines, but it didn't work. He was so upset and would often skulk around saying, "I'm a pilot without a plane." He didn't feel like he could do anything else with his life. Money was tight. Being a doctor didn't mean I was getting a good paycheck, but I was still willing to support him. I paid for him to go to school in business administration. While he was taking his classes, I worked three jobs, even though pregnancy made me vomit every day for the first three months.

I had to tell my parents I was pregnant. I didn't know what they would say.

My parents grew up during *La Violencia*, The Violence, in Colombia from 1948 to 1958, an uncertain and especially dangerous time in Colombia's history. Nobody was safe—it didn't matter who you were or what area you lived in. Historians say that the era my parents grew up in was the worst. My father grew up about three hours northeast of Bogotá, and my maternal grandmother grew up about three hours southwest of the city. Miles apart from one another, they all suffered the same fate.

During the late 1940s and well into the '50s, the two political parties were at war. It hit the Colombian countryside terribly, especially in areas where my father grew up. My dad, at the age of seven, witnessed people brutally murdered by machete. He often had to hide for long periods of time up in the mountains. Thousands of Colombians were killed—often the bodies left in the streets for days, mutilated and without dignity. Villages were burnt, women and children raped, and everyone robbed of their belongings, sanity, and security. The ones who survived were forced to abandon their homes and flee. Brutality was normal—a given, inevitable part of every single day. Living in that reality will break a person. For my father, it turned him cruel.

La Violencia is "officially" considered the most violent period in Colombian history, but Colombia has always been a violent canvas.

My childhood wasn't much different from *La Violencia.* The violence in those early years planted the seeds for future guerrilla militants who became organized terror machines by the time I was born. Trust does not exist in Colombia. In the United States, if you see someone hurt or passed out in the street, you assume they need help and call 911. In Colombia, you assume it is a trap. If you stop, you get mugged. If they are not faking it, most likely they were drugged and robbed, and you keep going, never stopping to help. If you stop to help, you could end up picking yourself off the street with your head bashed and bleeding and everything down to your shoes gone. And that's only if you could get up at all.

During my middle school years, when the violence had picked up in our area, my mother hired a neighbor to drive me and my sister to and from school to make sure we were safe. One day, we approached the car ready for school and found the driver slumped over. He was covered in vomit, reeked of alcohol, and looked dead.

We freaked out, thinking there was a corpse in our driveway. Even then, I was more disgusted than frightened. When we called the police, they said he had been drugged with scopolamine and robbed. He had no memory of the incident, but the view of his slumped body stayed with me for a while. I didn't want to get any more rides to school from him, but my parents didn't listen or even begin to take me seriously.

Looking over my shoulder was automatic, making sure

no one was coming to hurt me and my sisters. The military was at war with the guerrillas. Drug cartels were at war with each other. Assassinations and executions in broad daylight were common. Being outside of the big city was dangerous because guerrillas would initiate roadblocks, holding cars at gunpoint and taking whatever they wanted. Many families would be taken for ransom, often killed even if the ransom money was paid.

I didn't understand it at the time, but that constant threat of violence affected me. It taught me not to trust. The relentless state of danger during those years gave me a sense of a foreshortened future.

Even so, life went on.

School came easily for me. I immediately became the overachiever of my family. I couldn't control the insanity happening in my life—my father brutally beating my mom and my sister, my paternal aunt running over my dog with her car (on purpose), neighbors disappearing, a distant cousin in our family trying to touch me, or bombs going off in the city. All of that was just part of my everyday life. But I could control getting good grades. I could control having my teachers like me. Doing well in school was the only way I could control outcomes.

At first, I wanted to go on and study physics so I could become an astronaut and fly millions of miles away from Earth. Physics proved challenging during high school. I decided instead that I wanted to be a pilot. There was something about being in the sky. I could be closer to my brother and far from everything else. The Colombian Air Force didn't accept women back then, and I knew most commercial airlines wouldn't hire a seventeen-year-old girl, so I had to change my plans. Finally, I settled on studying medicine. Now I know it was also a desperate attempt to try to fix my mom, but then, it just seemed like a good option. I had the goal of moving overseas, leaving the violent past behind. I decided to take the US medical exams. I was never afraid of not achieving my goals—I knew I would.

My pregnancy did not make me lose sight of that.

I knew I had to tell my parents about my pregnancy individually. My dad worked away from home most of my life. He did what he was used to—escaping bad situations. He would come home to visit occasionally, always bringing us new clothes and always filled with anger for my mom. She had sunk into a deep depression when my brother died, and I guess my dad was trying to beat her back into normalcy. It didn't work. So he'd beat my sister tirelessly too.

My mom and sister were very passive, sweet, and afraid. My dad never hit me, but I guess it was because I was a little like him. I was aggressive and fearless—he knew I would fight back. Outside of the brutal beatings, my dad also had two children with another woman. He would flaunt this by telling my sister she was named after his mistress, a strange cruelty he found funny.

He has never admitted to any of his mistakes, and he has never addressed his own trauma. When he wasn't causing pain, he was always complaining about everyone who wronged him. From my mother and the doctors who couldn't heal her to his siblings and associates, everyone was out to get him. I was always grateful when he just left us alone.

To break the news of my pregnancy, I invited my dad out to lunch—something we rarely did. I told him in a public space so that he would mind his manners to some degree. I avoided him unless it was absolutely necessary. I knew he wouldn't suddenly become caring. He barely had any reaction at all, which was surprising as I was expecting an angry or even violent outburst.

When I told my mom I was pregnant, she said I'd screwed up my whole life.

She had her own painful reason for this reaction; perhaps she didn't want me to suffer the same loss she had.

After my baby brother died, she had her first of many admissions to the psychiatric unit for severe bipolar and anxiety disorders. She worried constantly, obsessing over every worst-case scenario. If one of us sneezed, she'd spiral into panic, convinced it was cancer, pneumonia, or some deadly infection. Her family didn't believe in mental illness, so they just said her behavior was a bunch of bad choices and a shitty attitude. They thought she just needed to "pull herself together." Our mother stayed for months at the hospital, and then we were sent to live with my grandmother.

The truth was, my mom was very sick. I had watched her unravel too many times not to know. Her episodes came in waves, unpredictable and exhausting. One week, she'd be full of wild energy, not sleeping, making big plans. The next, she'd sink into a fog, not showering, hardly speaking, getting out of bed only to try to kill herself. We never figured out what triggered the shifts, only that they came—and when they did, she disappeared behind them. Sometimes for weeks. Sometimes months.

My youngest sister was born when I was eleven, and from the very beginning, she was all light—smiley, calm, the kind of baby people love to hold. She had a softness about her that made me feel protective, especially with everything happening around us. Just a month after she was born, my mom slipped into one of her manic episodes and, out of nowhere, announced we were going on a "family vacation" to the Colombian coast. Dad was in Medellín working, and my mom had no intention of telling him the plan. The less Dad knew, the better. No planning, no packing—just a twelve-hour drive along winding cliffside roads with a newborn.

Somewhere high in the mountains, we pulled into a tiny roadside restaurant. The car had been struggling the whole way, and when we parked, it wouldn't turn off. Smoke started pouring out from under the hood—thick, black, and fast. The heat was stifling. My mom was laughing, belting out a song as if nothing was wrong, totally oblivious to the car sounding like it was going to explode.

My baby sister and our middle sister were still in the car. I knew we didn't have long before the whole thing could blow. My dad wasn't good for much, but he had taught me a few things about cars. I remembered enough to pop the hood and disconnect the battery. My hands were shaking, but I did it. Then I snatched open the door, grabbed my sisters, and held them close, heart pounding with relief.

I was only eleven years old.

My mom just kept singing.

So when it came time to tell my mom I was pregnant, I didn't know how she would react, because I knew from long experience that her reactions were never predictable.

We told Emilio's parents we were pregnant, and their reaction was the exact opposite of mine—ecstatic and immediately overbearing. It wasn't malicious—they were kind, generous people—but they didn't understand boundaries. My daughter would be their first granddaughter, and they took that as a divine calling. Once I married Emilio, I was absorbed into the family like water into a sponge. Immediately, his mother wanted to shop for baby clothes together.

His father called to check on me constantly. And every Sunday—without fail—we were expected to show up at his grandmother's house for hours of food, gossip, unsolicited parenting advice, and chaotic conversation with half the extended family.

I tried to go along with it, at first. I smiled. I let myself be wrapped into this web of family closeness. But I hated it. My own family was nothing like this—we barely talked and preferred to keep a safe distance, only interacting on holidays. Emilio's family was always there. They'd show up to our house at night without calling, just because they were in the mood to chat or drop something off. It felt like I could never breathe without someone from his side watching, helping, or inserting themselves into our lives. I knew they meant well, but their version of love felt like I was constantly being watched. It felt like I could not breathe, like they were suffocating me.

And then there was Emilio's dad, who had a medical opinion about everything. He treated my pregnancy like he owned it, like he was the one pregnant. From the moment we shared the news, he tried to take over, insisting I give birth at the hospital where his best friend worked, pushing his preferences for doctors, birthing plans, even names. His behavior pissed me the fuck off. He lacked boundaries—or even the understanding that boundaries were something he should have. He was accustomed to being the "decider" in his family, and they were used to deferring to him on most things. But I was the decider in my family, and I resented the hell out of being told when and how I would be having my child.

Emilio's family had also been affected by violence in Colombia. Several of his relatives had been kidnapped over the years—ripped from their homes, their lives held for ransom. The family learned to navigate terror like second nature, constantly paying people off to avoid being the next target. Violence didn't discriminate. It touched everyone—from educated professionals like Emilio's father to politicians, farmers, regular folk, and men like my dad, who had tried to outrun its reach.

Violence and escape were threads woven through both our family histories, etched into our genetic material, passed down through generations. It was inextricable from who we would live to be.

My mother's paternal family were Holocaust victims—most of them were killed in concentration camps during the war. Her father, my grandfather Friedrich, was one of the few who managed to escape. In 1938, he fled Nazi Germany just before the borders closed completely. I still don't know how he secured a Colombian visa—especially considering Colombia had an active Nazi chapter at the time that fought hard to keep Jewish refugees out—but somehow, he made it. He boarded a steamship from Hamburg and crossed the Atlantic, arriving alone in the humid port of Buenaventura. He lost contact with his entire family in the process. Years later, he would learn that his sister was murdered in Auschwitz, and his parents ended up in a Jewish ghetto in Shanghai. His brother, "Basti," emigrated to New York, but they were not close.

Friedrich never spoke of the past. In fact, he hardly spoke at all. What little I remember of him is his silence, broken only by abrupt demands for quiet, usually aimed at his kids or us grandkids. He had a sharp glare that made us sit still. I think maybe the noise inside his own mind was already unbearable.

The only person who seemed to bring him peace was my grandmother. She was a native Colombian woman who said she was a direct descendant of the Pijaos warriors—a fierce Indigenous tribe who lived in the Tolima region long before the Spanish colonizers arrived. The Pijaos fought bravely but were nearly wiped out. Their resistance was met with horrific brutality: People thrown to wild dogs, raped, enslaved, erased. But stories say they didn't cry out in pain. They met their deaths with their heads held high. Their original name for themselves was Pinaos, which meant "pride"—a name that fit their legacy much more accurately than the derivative Pijaos, which is the perverted Spanish name given to them from the Spanish *pija* or "dick," since Pinaos men did not cover their genitals. The perversion stuck, and "Pijaos" became what they called themselves, too. Their spirituality was deeply connected to nature, believing that dead Pijaos become deer in the next life.

The Pijaos' spirituality resonates with mine. I do not practice any religion, but as I learned about the world, I have been drawn to Buddhism, which is deeply connected to nature and the potential of rebirth. Perhaps that tendency is drawing my Pijaos native heritage from the dark spring of my unconscious mind. Besides, I would not mind being a deer in my next life or a house cat for that matter.

Of the few Pijaos who survived colonization, many were later killed during *La Violencia*. The violence never stopped—it just changed form.

I don't have many vivid memories of my grandparents, but one stands out: Friedrich dancing the waltz with my grandmother. He would rarely hold her hand, and he never kissed her in front of anyone—but watching him dancing to his Austrian tunes with her told me everything I needed to know. He loved her.

They did what they could to survive. My grandma used

to call our family *pate perro*, a Colombian slang that doesn't quite translate into English but means something like "stray dog feet"—always moving, never still. It wasn't said with pity; it was said with pride. Jewish people had to move. The Pijaos had to move. Colombian peasants move. Victims of violence don't get to settle. They survive by staying in motion.

My family never talked about the things they escaped. They were all very quiet and demanded that their children be the same. Hushed tones and buried emotions traveled from my grandparents' home to my parents' home and eventually to my own.

While my family remained silent and distant, Emilio's family had a front-row seat to my entire pregnancy—whether I wanted them to or not. It was challenging, not just physically but mentally and emotionally. I was constantly stressed, thinking about all the possible complications, questioning every ache and cramp. I was vomiting constantly. I couldn't hold down food, not even water some days. Within my first few months, I had lost nearly ten pounds, and since I only weighed ninety-eight pounds when I got pregnant, that weight loss was alarming. My family said I looked like a worm that had swallowed a green pea, all bones except for the swollen belly.

Making matters worse, Emilio's parents were everywhere. They tried to help, but their "help" often felt more like demands and judgment. I was desperate for space from them, to feel in control of my own pregnancy. They refused to let me. Emilio's father thought his job as a cardiologist somehow made him an expert in everything—including childbirth.

I told him, clearly and more than once, that I didn't want him in the delivery room. But when it came time to give birth, I was ignored. The umbilical cord had wrapped tightly around my baby girl, who was to be named Sofia, and I had planned a C-section. I was freaking the hell out, hurting and sweating, already worried my baby wouldn't survive.

And then, in the middle of it all, I heard the door slam open. Emilio's dad barged into the operating room like it was his living room. He started barking orders at the doctors and nurses as if they were his personal assistants. On my back, with too many bodies moving around me, I couldn't see him, but I could hear him clearly. His voice cut through everything: louder than the beeping machines, louder than the anxious thoughts racing through my head. All I could see was the bright red of my blood reflected in the surgical lights. No one told me what was happening, and the surgery was taking too long. All I could hear was him saying "Don't worry, don't worry," which did not reassure me in the slightest.

But I was worried. I was furious. I felt erased. I lay there, anxious and exposed, gritting my teeth through the pain and through the noise, knowing that this wasn't the way I had imagined meeting my daughter.

When my baby girl was finally born, the room went silent. She didn't cry—not even a whimper. Her skin was purplish blue, her tiny chest barely moving. I remember holding my breath, terrified that the worst had already happened. The medical team sprang into action, taking her away from me before I could even touch her. I caught one last glimpse of her wrinkled little body as they rushed her to the ICU. For the next twenty-four hours, I waited in a daze, staring at the ceiling, wondering if I would ever get to hold her. Once she managed to take in a bit of formula, they released her.

Giving birth felt strange. I carried her for nine months, and I could feel her moving inside me—an independent part of my body completely outside of my control. Then once she's born, here is this little stranger. When I finally saw her, there was nothing really to do but introduce myself. "Hi—I'm your mom. Nice to meet you, *bizcocho*." Biscuit.

CHAPTER 3

ENGLISH PLEASE

WHEN MY SISTERS WERE YOUNG, I watched over them because my mother was pretty checked out all the time, as if unaware we were even there. I was the one in control of keeping the house stable and my sisters alive. Though I was ever watchful and in control, I was not loving or nurturing. I exerted control the same way the German nuns did at the Catholic school I attended. They had no compassion, love, or softness for their charges—we were rigidly controlled with yanks to our ear lobes and twists of the arm. We learned it was either silence and compliance— or pain. In turn, I became a bully to my middle sister and friends, rigid and cold like the nuns. My middle sister, neglected by our parents, practically glued herself to my side, her only consistent guardian, and she suffered for it, as I lashed out and mistreated her to make her keep at least some distance from me.

When Sofia was a newborn, I had a tough time managing it all, and my youngest sister—only eleven years old—stepped in to help. She had the natural maternal instinct that I never really had. She was soft and nurturing in a way I never learned to be. She fed Sofia, changed her diapers, and rocked her to sleep. I had kept my sisters alive when they were babies, but all the affectionate stuff was out of my reach. Even with my sister's help, I struggled really trusting anyone with Sofia.

My mom's tendency to panic and the sudden loss of my baby brother had seeped into my unconscious, driving me to always maintain rigid control.

One night, I was convinced Sofia wasn't breathing right. I shook Emilio awake. "We need to get her to the hospital," I said, panicking. "Something's wrong."

I called my in-laws in the middle of the night, desperate for help.

"Sofia has respiratory problems," I blurted. "She might need a ventilator!"

"Calm down, Dolores," my father-in-law replied. I hated being told to calm down.

We brought her to the pediatrician the next day only to hear it was nothing but a stupid booger in her nasal passage. Nothing serious. I felt some relief, but soon I felt sure something was still wrong.

Although I occasionally called my in-laws for help, I didn't truly trust anyone around Sofia— not even them. I felt she couldn't be left alone because she might die. Sofia wasn't a difficult baby, at least not in the ways I had braced for. She wasn't rowdy or whiny. She didn't climb on dressers or scream throughout the night.

Even then, she was a peculiar little baby. I could see both me and Emilio in her face and her disposition. She was quiet, observing her surroundings passively. She was a picky eater and never drank from her bottle. She'd just blow air on it or push it away altogether.

It frustrated me. She was always on the lowest end of

the growth charts. Her pediatrician kept a close eye on her weight, always telling me to try this or that. Finally, I started adding a bit of chocolate powder to her formula. She gulped it right down from a sippy cup. From that moment on, chocolate became her weakness. To this day, she's a full-blown chocoholic. Her first word wasn't "*mama*" or "*papa*," it was "*conina*," her baby version of "a little bit of chocolate."

She seemed to be born already so fiercely independent that she came into the world with a Michelin-star palate, fully developed. She wasn't going to fuss with cheap milk. She had a taste for fine things from her first days.

When Sofia turned two, I went back to working long shifts at the hospital in Bogotá. I was still paying for Emilio to go back to school to study business management, and we were broke. I was often working over thirty hours at a stretch. I never slept. Even when Sofia slept through the night, I didn't. I'd lie awake listening to her cries or gasping breaths. We lived in a cramped apartment building with paper-thin walls, so every sound felt like a threat: a slammed door, a neighbor's TV, a cough down the hall. I rarely slept for more than a few hours.

Our apartment building was six floors high, with eight identical buildings all sharing a subterranean parking lot. The stairway had bars, but the gap was plenty wide enough for a two-year-old like Sofia to fall through. I pictured Sofia slipping right out of my grasp and dropping six stories to her death. I felt I couldn't truly trust anyone to watch for Sofia the way I could—and sometimes I felt proven right. I tried to trust in Emilio, but he was never as watchful or careful as I would be.

When I came back from work one day, the security guard stopped me with a comment.

"Sofia is so funny," he said, grinning.

"What do you mean?" I asked.

"She was out here earlier—with her shoes on the wrong feet."

I froze. "Just her?"

"Yeah. She fixed her shoes and went right back to the play park."

I couldn't even respond. Why the hell had Sofia been outside by herself? On the way up, I noticed every gap in that railing. I noticed every dark hallway that Sofia could be snatched down and disappear forever. I noticed every piece of litter that could have lodged itself in her throat. By the time I reached our floor, I was on the edge of throwing up and my chest ached.

When I opened the apartment, I found Sofia playing in the living room. I asked Emilio what the fuck had happened. He shrugged and said he must've dozed off. He confessed that he woke up with her knocking on the front door. He insisted it had only been a few minutes.

That couldn't have been true. My daughter, ever the independent mind, had probably not even tried to wake her dad, who was fast asleep. She just decided to go play at the park, got her shoes wrong, climbed down six flights of stairs, made it outside, played on the playground, adjusted her shoes, apparently had a whole fucking conversation with the security guard, got tired, found the right building again, climbed up six floors, and knocked on the door to be let in. She could've been snatched, run over, lost, eaten something poisonous, murdered, hit her head—any number of things.

It took me forever to catch my breath.

Because I knew exactly what could happen when you left a child alone. That's how we lost my little brother, Javiercito.

I remember that morning. I begged my mom to take me to the store to get some new shiny red shoes. She agreed and we left Javiercito with the housemaid so we could go shoe shopping. We shopped; I got my new red shoes. When we came home, there were cars filling the driveway. Every light was on in the house, so it was glowing. People were spilling out of the front door. I thought, *Wow, what a party.*

No one told me that my brother had died. He just disappeared. I never got to say goodbye.

Later, I found out that while we were shopping, the housemaid had left him alone to sleep, but Javiercito woke up and got tangled in the curtain cord. He was too little to cry for help and too weak and uncoordinated to disentangle himself on his own. He accidentally self-strangled and died.

My mother lost her mind, unable to cope with the reality of it.

After that scare with Sofia, I realized I couldn't keep doing things halfway—half-rested, half-paid, half-safe. I was stretched thin, emotionally, financially, and physically, and it felt like no matter how many hours I worked, we weren't getting anywhere. I didn't want Sofia to grow up in that cramped apartment with the shaky stairwell and the rusty playground.

By then, I could read and write in English, but I still couldn't understand spoken conversations. But that didn't deter me from the goal of passing the US medical licensing exams. In between diaper changes and hospital shifts, I hired a private English tutor to help me prepare for the interviews in the US. I wrote up what I expected the interview questions would be, and she helped me translate my answers. Week after week, we rehearsed until I could say my answers without thinking. I was determined to be clear and understood, showing that I could work in an American hospital, even if I was not yet fluent.

Sometimes, I thought about my mother. She had once been fluent in English—and even learned German, too, which she probably did just to feel closer to her father. She had loved languages before she lost her mind. Working toward my US medical license made me think of my mom, how smart she was, and how much I wanted to know how to heal her. Even when I was not thinking about it consciously, I carried all my experiences with her in my unconscious mind. I wanted to master what I could not do as a child: cure my mom once and for all.

That winter, I flew to the US for an interview in New Haven, Connecticut. I packed my bag, kissed Sofia goodbye, and flew out—completely unprepared for the East Coast winter weather. As soon as I got off the plane, the cold bit at me relentlessly. I didn't have a suitable coat or gloves, and I couldn't believe how powerful the cold was. I hurried to the Motel 6 I had booked.

The next morning, the cold had deepened even further, and there was a snowstorm. Freezing in my inadequate clothes, I took a train and then a taxi to the hospital. The interview itself went well. They asked every question I had practiced. I left the hospital confident that I had done what I came to do.

I made it back to the train station, but when I got off at my stop, there were no taxis. I waited at the uncovered plat-form, shaking and losing feeling in my extremities. The columns and awnings of the train station did nothing to keep out the elements. My fingertips were burning; my shoes were soaked through with the snow. I had no cell phone, so I tried every taxi number I could find on the station's pay phone, but either they wouldn't send a taxi out in the weather or didn't understand my developing English.

I was stuck at the train station for hours on the outskirts of the city, my exposure to the weather becoming increasingly dangerous with every passing minute. The station seemed so far from anything. All the passengers from the trains had gotten in their parked cars and driven off, paying no attention to me.

I didn't know what to do. As it was my first time in the US, I had no idea that calling 911 might have been an option, but I did know that if I stayed out in the cold, hypothermia would set in, and I would soon start to become confused. If I was unable to think clearly, I would be even less likely to find my way to the hotel and safety. My only choice was to start walking, though I had no idea which direction my motel was in.

After about half an hour, I saw a small row of houses. I couldn't keep going, so I rang the bell of the first one to ask for help. A man answered; his family was sitting down to eat dinner. I explained what had happened as best I could. They brought me inside to get warm, gave me dinner, and drove me back to the motel.

I was glad to have found help and safety in the end, but the whole experience made me suspicious and wary of New Haven. Between the blizzard and the taxis, New Haven itself seemed sketchy—I didn't know how to navigate such a place on my own. After being stranded for hours at the train station, I didn't want to ever see it again. Again, the unconscious was pushing me, and my fear of that train station directly influenced where I ended up in residency more than the interview I had rehearsed for. When Yale New Haven offered me a residency, I turned it down.

Instead, I accepted residency at a hospital in the Bronx.

I had a friend working there, and it seemed like a safer, more familiar option than New Haven. I'd heard stories about gangs and crime in the Bronx, but that was just life as far as I was concerned. Nothing could be worse than Colombia. So I packed up our few belongings and dragged Emilio and Sofia, who was four years old, onto the flight to emigrate to the South Bronx.

Without realizing it, I was also abandoning my sisters. I had been in many ways what kept the household going, even in chaos, and without me, they were left alone to deal with our broken parents on their own.

We landed in New York City in August of 2000 with seven suitcases of pots, clothes that would be next to useless when winter set in a few months later, and Sofia's favorite toys. We had about $700 to our name. Emilio was fluent in English, so I relied on him to navigate. I asked about the shuttle vans to Queens—where we'd be staying with my friend for a few days—but he shook his head. "They can't fit all the bags," he said. "We will have to take a limousine."

"What? A limo? That can't be. There must be another way!"

He disappeared into a pay phone booth and returned a few minutes later, calm and easygoing as usual. "It's on the way," he told me.

A little while later, a white limousine pulled up in front of us.

I stared at it like it had landed from another planet. The driver got out and started loading our bags. "How much is this going to cost?" I hissed at Emilio.

"Eighty dollars." He shrugged. "But it's the only way to get all of our things."

I was furious—eighty dollars is a lot when you only have seven hundred to your name—but I also didn't see another option and didn't have the English to ask myself. Emilio, in his excitement to be in America, was acting like a little boy instead of a man; he probably wanted to arrive in what he considered "style" without thinking at all about what we would truly need in the coming weeks and months. So I paid the man, climbed into the back, and held my breath as we inched our way through the tight streets of Queens. Every time we passed a parked car, I braced for the sound of metal scraping. A fat, shiny limo on a tiny street—how stupid. Suffice it to say, that was the only time I've ever been in a limo.

We then sublet a single room from a Colombian doctor who was a friend of a friend. She worked at a different hospital in the Bronx, so we almost never crossed paths. She charged us $600 for the room. Our space was about 80 square feet, just enough to wedge in a small-sized mattress where the three of us slept. There were mice that ran and scurried along baseboards. There was a closet in the corner that barely held our clothes, so we shoved our things in to fit. When the upstairs apartment sprung a leak, it drenched all our clothes. We wrung things out, hung them to dry, and kept using them, though they were forever stained after.

The stench of urine permeated the building, giving us all a perpetual ammonia headache. One day we discovered the source of the smell when the tenant on the first floor, and his thirty or more cats, was evicted.

Outside wasn't much better—sirens at all hours, people screaming, and drug dealers and prostitutes working openly on the corners.

It wasn't long before I felt I'd made a horrible mistake by dragging my family along. The South Bronx was grim, loud, and mean. In this part of the hemisphere, the eighty-five-year-old grandmas would use street drugs, and the children were unruly compared to what I was used to. The so-called "poor" wore expensive tennis shoes and golden neck chains. Elementary school children would carry explicit sex drawings in their backpacks. It was a different world.

Sofia hated it, especially the cold. Even when it was warm, she dreaded the cold she knew was coming, saying, "*Nos va a caer el invierno.*" Winter is going to fall upon us.

We ran out of money in the first month, and it was always a battle between Emilio and me. There were times when we only had coins for laundry, but my husband would spend them on ice cream for our daughter instead. To this day, I hate ice cream trucks; their loud, obnoxious music makes my whole neck and back tense and spasm.

Sofia was imitating what she saw every day around our apartment. *Well*, I thought, *we need to get the fuck out of here.*

CHAPTER 4

LIVING IN THE BRONX

LIVING in the Bronx was unforgiving. Everywhere was aggression and meanness, and it was making me mean too. There was no ease or room to breathe or find a comfortable pace for yourself that didn't require a constant, exhausting fight. If you ever stopped fighting, the Bronx would run you over. It was a hard place, and it made people who lived and worked there hard. After about a year, I had saved enough money to move us out.

We moved right across the George Washington Bridge to New Jersey. The neighborhood was called Fort Lee. I'd heard it was better—less dangerous, better schools, cleaner, and safe. We moved to a place where most of our neighbors were Korean. The neighborhood was calm. I no longer heard screaming and gunshots all night. Our street was clean, and our neighbors were considerate and educated. We had a one-bedroom apartment on the first floor of our building. No more lugging groceries up flights of stairs.

Sofia made friends with three Korean children from her school. The family didn't live near us—they lived in a different, luxurious building. I'd heard that Celia Cruz even lived there.

Ethan, one of the kids from the Korean family, really liked Sofia. He gifted her one of his sister's Barbies without telling her or his parents. Sofia loved it. The next day, he came back with clothes, shoes, and accessories, per Sofia's request.

I was relieved Sofia was making friends.

Work was exhausting, draining me of all I had in me. In the Bronx, you swam or you sank. The city hospital in the Bronx was tough. There was a police station inside the hospital because the patients would usually get violent. I saw patients try to stab nurses, try to off themselves in front of us—all types of horrific moments. The hospital was affiliated with Cornell University and was run by immigrant doctors who had been specialists in their countries. Most of them were from India. There was only one white American doctor in the whole place, and he was completely dysfunctional, which I found shocking for a city hospital.

The competition was fierce among the doctors. You could feel the tension in the air. The patient care was intense. Many of the patients abused drugs and had AIDS. Injuries and illness were constantly complicated by rampant drug addiction. Blood needed to be drawn every six hours, but their veins were damaged from drug use. When I couldn't get a vein in their hand or arm, I'd have to draw blood in their tiny toe veins. I would have to squint and get so close to their feet—it was a very difficult task, and the risk of getting stuck with needles in the process was always too high.

I was still learning English, so I communicated awfully slowly, and my accent was very heavy. Some of the nurses would call me names that were not in the dictionary, like the c-word. All of the nurses were either Filipino or African American. Some of the nurses were pretty nice, but others were nasty and mean to Latinos. There were only about eight of us Latinos, and we were at the bottom of the caste system. The whole experience was painful. From the culture shock to the hours, I was miserable. I hated internal medicine. I could not trust my coworkers.

And I couldn't even defend myself against the name-calling and rudeness because I didn't know English well enough. The work environment was unsafe, and I couldn't do my best to help people there.

After several months, I realized I was beginning to dream in English. Things became somewhat easier for me when I could dish English curses back; I could show the others that I was not one to fuck with. But the grueling hours and the endless line of senseless injuries and violence wore on me, as well as the steady stream of disrespect. I probably complained about that damn hospital every day.

One day, Sofia looked up at me earnestly. She had developed her dry frankness at a very early age, and she asked, "*¿Y porque tienes que ir a ese hospital todos los días si te tratan como una mierda?*" Why do you keep going back to that hospital where they treat you like a piece of shit?

After a year, I was finally moved to a new assignment in the inpatient psychiatric unit located on the tenth floor. It was September of 2001. My in-laws came to visit, and they had planned to take my daughter to the World Trade Center on September 11th. It was 8:30 a.m. when the chaos started, and the planes hit the towers. I was shocked to see that the violence and chaos had followed me. Patients were screaming at the windows. We could see the smoke coming off the Twin Towers. Sirens blared all around us. None of the phones worked. I couldn't call my family to know if they were okay.

Luckily, Emilio and his parents were never on time. They had planned to be at the World Trade Center early in the morning, but all of them constantly ran late. It normally drove me crazy, but that day, it saved my child. I was stuck in the hospital for days.

Bomb threats forced us to evacuate then return over and over as the chaos continued. I don't remember being afraid, just upset that tragedy would always find me.

Emilio still didn't have a job. He did nothing with his degree in business administration. All he ever wanted to be was a pilot. He would sleep through interviews all the time. I even paid for flight classes so that he could complete the minimum number of flying hours needed for airline jobs. We did not have money to pay for a babysitter, so sometimes Emilio would take Sofia to his flying lessons. His instructor would turn off an engine, simulating power failure, even while Sofia played with her Barbie in the back seat of the plane.

After 9/11, though, all of the commercial airlines stopped hiring foreign pilots. He was a pilot with no plane again. I still felt somewhat protective of his dream of being a pilot. Now I know it was because that was my only connection to my little brother, but at the time, I just blindly supported.

Emilio never had a vision for the future. Years later, after completing my specialty training, I was working several jobs, barely sleeping, and sometimes I'd check our accounts, and we'd be in the negative. I'd ask what happened, and he would shrug his shoulders and say he'd bought a pair of $300 shoes. I would try to get him to help around the house. I'd make lists for him: Here's what we have to do, and here's what we have to pay. When I came home from working twelve-hour days, he'd say he didn't have time to do anything because he was at the gym.

I was in charge of everything. I was upset all the time. My fists were always balled up with tension. I gritted my teeth constantly. When I spoke, it normally came out snappy and aggressive. I couldn't understand why I was always so angry. Now, I know it was because Emilio and I were constantly in a state of resistance—trying to row the same boat in two opposite directions. I felt like I was stuck. But back then, all I knew was that it was just my life.

Sofia became even more independent. She really followed in my footsteps of keeping to herself and just getting things done. Sofia is proof that your genes and circumstances affect how you raise your kids.

When I was young, I learned to be quiet. Without even realizing it, I taught Sofia the same. One day while in the Bronx, Sofia was super upset. I don't remember what happened, but she wouldn't stop screaming. She was crying and yelling nonstop. Neither of us could calm her down. I kept saying, "Sofia, calm down. Sofia, hush. Sofia, stop." I thought for sure someone would call the police and say we were hurting her. I couldn't let that happen. She just kept going and going. Then it was like instinct—I grabbed her and took her to the shower. I turned on the cold water and voilà. It worked like magic. Her clothes were soaked, and she looked shocked, but the tantrum stopped. Emilio looked terrified.

"What? I'm not hitting her. She isn't going to die, and the tantrum had to stop," I said.

I didn't even think before doing it. It was instant—I was

repeating what I'd seen. My grandparents were allergic to noise. When we went to their house, we had to be silent. They made it clear: Do not scream; do not talk loudly. If one of us did, my grandma would take us to the wash basin. It was made out of cement, and the water was always frigid cold. She'd stick us in there, and we'd go quiet. You can't scream when you're in shock from the cold. I had repeated that pattern with Sofia. Years later, when Sofia was already grown up, we were talking about it.

"I better keep quiet now—God forbid you give me the shower treatment," said Sofia.

I thought, *Oh God, how awful.* I apologized to her and explained how I was just carrying out learned behaviors. It's difficult to escape those patterns because it's wired into your brain, and you just do it without thinking. That part of my parenting wasn't my brightest moment, but it only happened once, thankfully. Sofia didn't throw any more tantrums after that. Interestingly enough, nowadays, Sofia likes cold plunges, her own version of cold-water therapy.

While I was stressed out working at the city hospital, my weight dropped again. I was only eighty-five pounds. It used to feel like my heart was skipping beats, like I was choking. Back then, I seriously thought I was dying. Now, I know it was panic attacks.

Every night, I'd take the subway home. It was always during the late hours, after midnight. There were scary people on the train at that time. Each ride, I'd just sit there, wondering how my life had unraveled so quickly. I was certain I'd made a huge mistake leaving Colombia. I had snatched Emilio away from the comfort of his family, his routines, his life. And for what? We had no money. No stability.

Then came the sickness. As an immigrant you get tested

for tuberculosis when you first arrive. I tested positive, though I suspected it was a false positive from the BCG vaccine we all got as children in Colombia to prevent tuberculosis. But the hospital didn't consider it a false positive, even though I had no symptoms. They pushed me into a harsh treatment regimen, and soon my skin yellowed. I had developed hepatitis from the medication. I was exhausted, nauseous, and rail-thin from constantly throwing up. I went to the ER one day. A nurse glanced at my chart then at me and asked bluntly, "What street drugs are you on? Do you have HIV?" Her words smacked me. I sobbed. It was all too much. I felt like I was drowning in a country that was supposed to be my new beginning.

In the Bronx, we enrolled Sofia in a Jewish school—not because we were Jewish, but because it seemed like the best option among the limited choices we had. It was organized and clean. On paper, it was a good school. Some of her teachers were kind, patient, and genuinely cared about her learning. But others were downright cruel. During Sofia's first grade, there was one teacher who made a habit of shaming her in front of the entire class. Whenever her desk was messy, this teacher would dump the entire contents onto the floor in front of everyone. Pens, papers, notebooks —all scattered as the other kids watched.

Another teacher filled her head with nonsense, telling her things like, "Don't eat bread or you'll get fat." A different teacher even planted the idea that chores were a form of child abuse. "You should refuse to do housework unless your mother pays you," she told her. When Sofia protested about doing her chores, I simply told her to do them and ignored her demand for payment. *Eso no aplica a los Colombianos.* Those rules don't apply to us Colombians. She was upset and confused.

Sofia stopped talking—completely—for almost a year after we arrived in the US. She barely said anything at school or at home. And then, one day, she opened her mouth and started speaking English. No more Spanish. Bilingualism shows up in funny ways. Just like that.

The same year, my grandma died. There was no way for us to travel to Colombia for the funeral. I kept missing funerals, and honestly, I was relieved. It took me years to realize it, but death freaked me out ever since I lost Javiercito when I was a kid. I wanted no part in the rituals, no crowds, no church, no whispered prayers, no family gathering in mourning. I preferred to keep death at arm's length, pretending if I didn't look at it, maybe it wouldn't see me either. Unfortunately, my job was filled with death and suffering. I saw people die from gunshot wounds, stabbings, drug overdoses, and suicides.

I did make one friend in the hospital, though. He was a urologist from Cuba who was a psychiatry resident in the Bronx at the time. He called me *"flaca,"* the skinny one. His first name was Jesus. One day, I was helping on the neurology floor. I couldn't find a vein in one of the patients.

"*Flaca,* how are you doing with that vein?" he asked.

I was almost crying. "I can't get it. I have so much to do!"

Jesus came over and helped me out.

"Don't worry about it. Here's your sample," he said as he passed me the vial of blood.

Jesus himself had come to help me. If that was a sign from above, I completely missed it.

"I want to switch to psych," I blurted out. I had seen how the doctors and nurses on the psych floor were calmer, happier. I remembered my round of clinicals in the psychiatric ward. It was humane, a place where I could do good work and help people.

"Let me ask my program director. I think we have an opening," he responded.

I hoped it would work out. I was tired of drawing blood. I hated fluids. I had hated them all my life—any type of fluid. It was just disgusting. I couldn't do it anymore.

CHAPTER 5

THE ALLURE OF PSYCHIATRY

MY FIRST EXPERIENCE with a psychiatric ward was during medical school rotations.

Walking into the psychiatric hospital was immediately different from any other medical environment I'd experienced. Everyone was so relaxed. I ventured into the patient garden, and it was hard to know who was a doctor and who was a patient. I liked how the doctors dressed—no lab coats, just corduroy pants, pleated jackets, and typically unruly hair. The residents there were all into the humanities and arts. They lived more freely, not afraid of taboos. Every week, they would meet at a bar to hang out after work. Out of all the areas of medicine I'd worked in, psychiatric doctors were the only ones I saw being friends and hanging out outside of work. They seemed to understand one of my favorite metaphors for life—we're all in the same skillet. Depending on where you are in the skillet, you might get exposed to varying degrees of heat, and even at the same temperature, some humans remain raw; only a select few get sautéed to a crisp perfection, and most of us get charred.

As I took it all in, a patient approached me.

"What's your name?" he said.

I told him "Dolores," which he repeated and added, "*Dolores, amarte debe ser toda una locura.*" Dolores, loving you would be complete madness. I couldn't contain my laughter. He was right. Even back then, at only nineteen or twenty years old, part of me could appreciate the authentic feel of a psychiatric unit.

During that rotation, I was fascinated by how the mind controls the body. I was able to observe some psychoanalytic sessions, where doctors and students could witness the unconscious mind at play. Students sat in the back of the room, just flies on the wall. There was one patient who could not use his right arm for years. He had uncontrollable tremors. Neurologists had ruled out Parkinson's disease and similar movement disorders, but his hand continued to shake. They told him that there was nothing medically wrong with him and sent him over to psychiatry.

As we observed his sessions, I noticed that he referred to himself as *el pájaro*, the bird, all the time. Growing up in Colombia, I knew that was code for a hitman. After a few sessions, the patient admitted that he had indeed been a hitman. He had killed nearly a thousand people, and the guilt was living in his hand that never stopped trembling. He could never bring himself to state directly that he killed people, only that he "took care of them for *el patrón*" (the boss). He was blind to the connection between his handgun grip, his guilt, and the tremors, but his body punished him anyway. Now retired, his shooting hand was completely useless.

I was fascinated by psychiatry, but I didn't want to get very close to it. Now, I realize I was coping in the same way, avoiding pieces of my past. The trauma of being surrounded by violence stuck with me, and I was not fully conscious of how I carried it in my body and in my choices. During medical school, and for years after, I kept avoiding it, sometimes consciously and other times unconsciously. I blocked out what I couldn't face and accept, and I avoided the pain as much as I could.

My time studying psychiatry in Colombia showed me the difference between memorizing what I was learning, which is what I did with other disciplines, and reflecting on what I was learning. I internalized psychiatry and partially applied it to my own life. Our psychiatry instructors had us do different activities like write poetry and essays, watch movies, and find hidden themes, meaning, and connections in what we were witnessing in the patients. One time, our professor asked us to write an essay about fantasy. I don't remember much of what I chose to write about, but I know it had to do with flying and jumping out of a plane, and the moment the parachute exploded open. I was proud of my writing, which felt true and honest to me in a way I couldn't quite explain. I had to read the essay out loud to the class. When I was finished, I looked over at my professor who was grinning.

"This sounds just like an orgasm," he said.

I was mortified. At the time, I had never had one of those. I couldn't believe he said that. There were no hard, unspoken limits in psychiatry; you were free to say whatever came to mind, no taboos, just understanding and acceptance.

Maybe part of me knew even then that I would eventually end up in psychiatry. For several years, I tried to avoid it. Now, thirty years into the field, I know it's because I was afraid working in psychiatry would take me on a path to facing my shit. I wanted to heal my mom, and I held onto so much sorrow from not being able to. My sorrow was in the driver's seat, controlling a lot of my actions without me even knowing it. Sometimes, it takes that long to address wounds. It can feel like opening a submerged chest that has been kept under tons of pressure while you surf miles above it. I kept delaying opening the chest until eventually, all the junk popped out. I can now examine the contents without breaking apart, but I was never eager to go on that journey because I knew breaking apart would be a necessary part of the work.

I avoided becoming a psychiatrist and tried internal medicine and neurology instead. I had to exhaust all other options first.

The Bronx helped with that. In that environment of constant strain, aggression, and struggle, I could never catch my breath. I switched from internal medicine to psychiatry in 2001. We stayed in New York a bit longer, then in 2002, we moved to New England so I could complete my training at a different hospital. New England was much calmer than New York.

The hospital in New England was better organized and well-run than the Bronx. The staffing was adequate, and the schedule made sense and was stable. The patients, who were generally more economically secure, showed up for their appointments on time. One patient came consistently for psychotherapy every week for two years straight, until one day he stopped showing up. This patient tended to be very timid and passive. He had battled depression all his life. He was tiny, thin-framed, and short, barely visible if he stood sideways. All the women in his life would mistreat him, starting with his mother, then all his girlfriends; it was a common tale of an abused man. He never missed an appointment and normally got to the hospital thirty minutes early. At least once a week, he would also call to confirm his appointment. He was polite, decent. My supervisor picked up on the fact that I didn't particularly like the patient, but he did not say that to me, and I was unaware of my feelings towards him.

"I want you to write a description of your patient. Just describe what you see," instructed my supervisor.

I started writing. I saw him as this minuscule man. I described him as a bug. Almost invisible, crawling around— just a creature asking to be crushed. I understood through the writing why my supervisor asked me to go through the exercise. It made me aware that a big part of me really disliked how he would never stand up for himself. A core-deep sense of frustration was growing inside me, away from my awareness. I realized that I needed to process those feelings to make sure I did not end up reacting the same way as the other women in his life.

Every week, this man came in and told me about his mother's physical abuse of him, his girlfriend mistreating him, and his neighbor's harassment. I listened to him and tried to empathize with his suffering. My job was to reflect back the pattern I was seeing so that he could feel empowered to change and break the cycle. He had one house in the city and another one in the countryside. His neighbors in the countryside were sketchy. He said they were addicted to drugs and would vandalize his house when he wasn't there. In an act of senseless cruelty, they killed his horse. He contacted the police, and they weren't helpful. So he put a few cameras up.

One day, he mentioned that he was going to get a gun for self-defense. I worried that he was planning on killing himself. I also asked the patient directly, and he denied any suicidal or homicidal ideation. I met with my supervisor weekly and, oftentimes, we talked about this patient. That week, I told my supervisor that I was concerned the patient might end up harming himself. Because there were no active threats to self or others, my supervisor said there was not much else we could do but to keep on exploring his thoughts about the gun in further sessions.

The patient stopped showing up for appointments. Two months went by, and I never heard from him, which was completely uncharacteristic. After two years of seeing him every week, I felt sick, thinking perhaps he had killed himself or the neighbors had killed him with his own weapon. Though my supervisor told me to wait and see what happened, I called him several times with no answer. Then, three months later, I got a letter postmarked from jail, and it was a note from my patient.

Dear Dr. Furtch: I just wanted to let you know that I am okay. Thank you for all of your help. Thanks to you I finally stood up for myself. The neighbors came to rob me, and I killed three of them. I decided no one else was going to step over me. For the first time in my life, I stood my ground, and I feel great. Don't worry, you're not in trouble. I told my lawyer that you are a great doctor.

He had killed his neighbors. All I could think was—*fucking hell!!!* I never anticipated this outcome. People are damned unpredictable. I could scarcely imagine him raising his voice at anyone, much less killing three people. I guess, in a way, he made a breakthrough. But at what cost? I wanted to respond, even though my supervisor urged me not to. I had been there for him for two years, and I felt compelled to reply. In the end, I wrote him a short and simple note telling him that I understood and hoped things would work out for him the best that they could, given the circumstances.

I still have his letter buried in a box in the attic. A reminder of how people can surprise themselves.

When we first moved to New England, Emilio picked up a job at a local supermarket. He would work a few hours there throughout the week when he wasn't working out. One day, he came home from work with a little kitten. She was only three or four weeks old. Sofia instantly fell in love with the cat. I never even had a chance to say we couldn't afford to keep it. Sofia named the kitten Lilly Ann Cadilly, which is a sweet name for such a feral cat. She was bright orange, her fur sticking up on all sides of her little body. She loved to climb the walls and slept curled up next to Sofia every single night. She was sneaky and would try to escape out of the front door when we were leaving for work or school. We'd all have to back out of the house to leave, ensuring we were watching the door as we closed it and could grab Lily's tiny body if she tried to scurry out.

One day, when Lilly was around two years old, Sofia and I were getting ready for my graduation ceremony. Emilio fell asleep on the couch, snoring lightly, while Sofia and I finished styling our hair. We went to the graduation and came home around 11 p.m. Sofia was already calling for the cat as soon as we walked in the door. Lilly didn't come. We searched the living room and bedroom for her but found nothing. Then I noticed a window was open with enough space for a kitten to wiggle through. Emilio had opened it, which we didn't do often because of Lilly's frequent escape attempts. He had accidentally forgotten to close it before we left.

Our apartment was on the third floor, and somehow Lilly managed to shimmy her way out and down. I peered out the window and saw no sign of the cat. I was grateful she wasn't splattered on the ground beneath the window. We searched for Lilly. We looked everywhere. Our building was near the woods, so we took flashlights and searched between the trees, waving flashlights and yelling for Lilly. Sofia was crying, worried so much for the mischievous cat.

About two hours into our search, we decided to check inside one of the other buildings at the apartment complex. There was Lilly, sitting in the middle of the corridor, just looking at us. I have no clue how she scaled down the three stories of our building. Or how she got into the other building with multiple locked doors, but there she was. All I could think about was the time when Sofia had also managed to wander away while Emilio slept, utterly unconcerned.

Sofia ran to her, and the cat let her pick her up to carry her home. Lilly became the most important being in Sofia's life, perhaps even more important than me or her father. That cat was her everything, and she lived twenty-one years. She was smart and naughty. She was a master in daring and successful escape attempts. The first one in New England set the tone for many more nights of searching for Lilly in whatever city we were living in.

Sofia had found comfort with her cat, and I had found some comfort in my career as a psychiatrist. My very first experiences with psychiatrists were the ones who worked with my mom when she was hospitalized. They tried to help her. Medications were either not effective, or she would stop taking them due to terrible side effects. She had to change meds often, but none of them worked. After we lost Javiercito and the abuse from my dad continued, it was like my mother could never recover.

One of my mother's psychiatrists asked me once if I was

depressed. He probably observed the signs. I was just a kid, so I didn't understand the question or why he would ask it, so I just said no. I've always been disciplined, but also anxious, ill-tempered, and impulsive. I could be empathetic, selfless, and helpful. I could also be mean and vindictive.

I never noticed those changes in my mood until I became a psychiatrist. I was just going through life until it hit me, and I had to self-reflect. I was aware that I wasn't happy and I could never relax. But I was also so busy that I did not have time to think about my inner self, and life wasn't giving me time to slow down. The unconscious mind is filled with all our unresolved issues. It influences all our behaviors more than we realize or often want to accept. Eventually, you must decide whether you want to resolve the issues, or you can just continue reacting the same way forever and accept the suffering that comes with it.

Eventually, I left my role in New England for a new position in the South. We all picked up and moved again. The South was hot and humid all the time, a welcome change from the cold.

My job at the state hospital was very challenging. All of the patients were extremely sick, and the units were under-staffed. I still wasn't sleeping well, even though Sofia was hyper-independent. A few years into my job, a patient hit me and gave me a black eye. I didn't want to go back to the hospital, but I had no choice. Emilio's reaction surprised and disappointed me—he simply shrugged it off, as if this was no big deal and something I should be able to ignore or accept, even while I was still in pain from the assault. I knew I didn't deserve to feel unsafe in my daily work, and I needed him to understand that too. He spent most of his days being a stay-at-home dad, getting Sofia to and from school, occasionally working part-time and helping a bit around the house. He always had trouble taking anything seriously, living in the moment to the extreme, never considering what he could learn from the past or what in the future he might need to prepare for. That was just part of who he was and still is.

At that time, Emilio was working part-time as a Spanish teacher. One day, he announced he had been invited to teach Spanish classes on a fancy, five-star cruise line. They told him that he wouldn't be paid, but he could go on the cruise for free and bring a plus one. It was a three-week-long cruise. The cruise was set to go from New York down the southeast coast of the US, then to Colombia, Cartagena, and the Panama Canal before finally heading up the Pacific to Mexico and California. It sounded amazing. I needed the break, so I took off work, and we left Sofia with a friend.

Since Emilio had started training to become a firefighter, he had started drinking protein shakes constantly to bulk up before his physical test. He had always been very thin and felt like he needed to be bigger before the test. We were packing for the cruise, and I saw him pouring tons of vanilla protein powder into Ziploc bags.

"We are Colombian. You know what that looks like, right?" I said.

"You're always thinking of the worst," Emilio replied.

"We are going to Mexico and Colombia. Bringing that is stupid. Just please don't."

"You're always telling me what to do," he complained.

I threw my hands in the air and gave up. He brought the powder in those suspicious little bags.

As I knew would happen, one of the cleaners, who was very young, found traces of the powder on a side table and quietly reported us to the security crew. We were walking around the ports, and I whispered to Emilio that we were being followed. He told me I was paranoid and couldn't relax. I could feel something was up, though. On the last day of the cruise, everyone had to pack their bags and leave them by the door for staff to collect. They told us we didn't have to. I kept telling Emilio something wasn't right. We went to breakfast in the morning, and when we got back to our cabin, I went to the restroom. As I flushed, I heard the door slam open.

There were police dogs. The whole ship was being emptied. The Border Patrol searched our cabin, holding us at gunpoint.

"Get out and against the walls! Hands up, NOW!" said the agent.

I glared at Emilio.

"You don't know that this has anything to do with me," he said.

Of course it did. The agents found the protein powder and nothing else, so they just left. But everyone on the ship knew what had happened. They all had to evacuate while our room was searched. It was embarrassing, and I was pissed.

I called a lawyer friend when I got home to see if I could file a lawsuit for discrimination. She said I didn't have a case because they had probable cause. Emilio was fired. He claimed he didn't know why. *Tremendo idiota.* Tremendous idiot.

CHAPTER 6

RELEASING THE ANCHOR

SOFIA WAS a good student all throughout school. After she overcame the barriers of living bilingually, she grew into a young woman who could fit in everywhere by being fluent in Spanish, English, and French. It was her gift to be able to adapt and find her place wherever she was. So we weren't surprised when she got into a university in Scotland. She was my daughter, after all—of course she wanted to travel far away. *Pate perro* until the end.

Emilio and I were proud of her, and the three of us traveled to Scotland to move her in. Getting to the university was a long trip. We flew from South Florida to London for a connecting flight to Edinburgh. Then we had to take a train before catching a bus and finally arriving in St. Andrews. Everyone there had red hair—even the cows. I realized Sofia wanted to be as far away as possible from the hot and humid southeast, and maybe from me. I was happy she chose Europe. I didn't have to worry about her being a school shooting victim there.

The town of St. Andrews is very old. The building her

dorm room was in looked like a castle. She wouldn't have to worry about having a car—everything was walkable. I knew she would do well there.

While we were there, we decided to do some sightseeing. We really enjoyed Stonehenge. I enjoyed getting to explore on my own for a few hours.

Leaving Sofia at the university was easy at first. I was excited and proud. But as soon as I sat down on the flight back, I started weeping nonstop. I was going to miss her so much, and I wondered what kind of mom would leave her child on another continent so far away. What if she got sick? What if something bad happened? What if there was an emergency? I thought about all the terrible things that could happen. She could get hit by a car on her way to class. Or she could get raped leaving a bar. She could fall off a cliff or drown in the North Sea. I was full of worry and picturing possible calamities—very on-brand for me.

Emilio, on the other hand, was chill as always. He loved Sofia but never worried about her the way I did. He sat on the plane and dozed off as usual, totally relaxed from the little trip.

When we arrived back in the United States, we had to pass through customs since we had been out of the country.

"Do you guys have anything to declare?" asked the agent.

"No," I started to say, when Emilio interrupted.

"Well, yes, we do," he said.

"What the fuck are you talking about? What did you buy?" I asked.

"Some bagpipes," he said.

I looked at him with blatant disbelief. Why the hell did he need bagpipes?

"When did you buy those? And with what money?!"

Emilio shrugged.

"Are you two related?" asked the customs agent.

"Not for long," I snarled back.

The bagpipes were $1,000, which he, of course, bought with a credit card. I had already been thinking heavily about leaving him. It had been years of the same thing—taking care of him. His problems with disorganization, carelessness, and impulsiveness made me conclude he had ADHD, but he didn't want to see a doctor and told me to just prescribe him something. I urged him to get on some meds so he could focus and get things done. Sometimes he would improve a little—take out the trash a few times or even manage to get a job. But he never kept them. Every single year, I would tell him if he didn't get his shit together, we would go our separate ways. I felt sad about the idea of us separating, but we had such different priorities. I felt like I was trying to drag him along. It was like pulling on an anchor that was stuck three feet deep in the mud. Impossible.

I never wanted to kick him out, though. I thought it would be too difficult with me working so much. I didn't want Sofia to suffer. I thought she would struggle if we weren't all together. Plus, Emilio was the one who handled all of her driving. It wasn't just taking her to school. Sofia was involved in a million extracurricular activities, and my work schedule didn't allow me to take her or pick her up. I couldn't imagine having to do that alone while working so much. It would be a disaster. Plus, I didn't have time for all the divorce paperwork.

But now, Sofia was away at college, and it was time for a change. I told Emilio that time was up. I had been telling him for over ten years how unhappy I was and how frustrating it was to feel like I didn't have a partner. It felt like I had a son instead, someone to supervise and take care of. He refused to leave. Instead, he just pretended everything was fine and kept going to the gym and spending money without even checking the accounts. I couldn't even think about savings because Emilio made it to where we never made it out of the red. I tried to give him another deadline for finding a job and moving out. I kept extending the deadline as he kept not doing what he needed to. He ignored me and played his bagpipes loudly and terribly. *El muy cabrón.* The bastard.

At the time, I was working several jobs to make ends meet. I'd come home and check our bank account, and we'd be in the red. The trash bin would be overflowing. And Emilio would just be sitting on the couch.

"Emilio, how is it possible that we are always in the red?"

"Oh, I needed some sneakers," he would say casually, wearing expensive clothes and shoes. Meanwhile, I did not care about name brands or labels. I just wanted comfortable, practical, and unassuming outfits. We were total opposites in that way. He wanted attention-grabbing, name-brand clothing, even when we had no money. I kept telling him that we needed to get out of red, but he never listened.

"I can't keep living like this. Please find a job so you can save your salary and move out," I'd say.

"You're never going to divorce me because you cannot cook. You'll die of hunger. You need me," Emilio would respond. I didn't need the reminder about my cooking skills. When Sofia was five, she stood her ground and politely set a plate of pancakes I made her to the side and said, "I refuse to eat Mama's food."

So, he was partially right. I couldn't cook well. I only

knew the basics, but thankfully, you can just subscribe for weekly meals from local restaurants. Plus, there was a Cuban restaurant nearby that had daily lunch deals and plenty of things to keep me fed. I still wanted him gone.

Emilio had turned into my son, or perhaps my baby brother. I couldn't save Javiercito, so I tried to save Emilio—always making sure he was safe, well-fed, clothed, and taken care of. We didn't feel like a married couple. We were barely attracted to each other. Once I saw the pattern of me taking care of him and how it had been holding me back, I knew I needed to get out. But I had been sucked into it by then, ensconced in a way that couldn't be easily undone. We were married for almost twenty years, so pretty much everything we did was just on autopilot at that point.

We had gotten married in Colombia, not the United States. I knew I'd have to pay for everything in the divorce because Emilio didn't have any money. The paperwork was one thing, but trying to figure out what to do with the house (which we owed way more on than it was worth), how to change the will, and so many similar things, were things I hadn't dealt with yet.

But I finally did it. I had saved a good amount of money for him in a retirement account so he wouldn't leave totally empty-handed. I ended up hiring a lawyer from Colombia that my friend recommended. It cost me $3,000, and we did everything virtually. I told him that we had nothing. Each of us had old cars, so Emilio would get his and I would keep mine. I had been telling Emilio to look for another place to live. He kept procrastinating, and I kept telling him his time had run out.

Emilio wouldn't leave until one day he read my text messages to a close friend. We had been friends since we were sixteen, and she had recently gotten divorced after realizing her husband was a deadbeat too. I was texting her about how excited I was to sleep with hot guys once Emilio finally left. She knew how I had taken care of him for years and was encouraging me to go for it. Neither of us ever cheated on our husbands, but I knew once Emilio left, I would be ready to get out and date again. I had told my friend I was getting older and ready to have "wild sex" for the first time.

When Emilio saw the messages, he was pissed.

"So you just want to, I don't know, fuck other people?" he said.

"What are you talking about?" I responded.

He waved my phone in the air. "I just read your texts."

"That's mine, and that is private. Give it back."

"That's it. I'm leaving!"

Emilio moved out later that day. I don't know how he got a U-Haul so quickly, but he parked it out front and started moving his things out. He packed everything in a fit of rage and rushed. All of our neighbors saw him. Our neighborhood was mostly Hispanic, and we are gossipy people by nature. I knew they'd all noticed the U-Haul in the cul-de-sac and were peeking out their windows to see what would happen. *Chisme fresco.* Fresh gossip.

Emilio left trash all over his bedroom. We had been sleeping in different rooms for years. He snored too loudly. We were like roommates—except he never paid his half of the rent. I was in disbelief that he actually left. I had been telling him for months to find a place to stay, but he never did. I have no idea where he slept those first few nights.

It felt like a weight had been lifted from my shoulders. I was so happy I had cut the line. The anchor wasn't sinking me anymore. I was upset he left his room trashed, but it was to be expected. He had been leaving messes for me to clean up for almost twenty years. I knew my neighbors had been watching because when I went to take out the trash the next day, one of them approached me.

"Oh, hello. I just wanted to introduce myself. My name is Josh," he said.

I had seen him a few times before. I knew he was divorced and had a few kids. I was surprised to see him at my door. I had just been venting to my friend about how I was nervous about meeting new guys, and where would I meet them? And yet, there I was, twenty-four hours after Emilio left, with a man at my front door.

"I saw your husband packing stuff into the moving truck, and I was wondering if that was temporary or..." he questioned.

He was pretty hot. I had seen him doing jumping jacks shirtless in front of my house almost every day.

After a few days, Emilio and I were able to talk calmly. I told him that we both knew things weren't working out.

"You deserve to be with someone who makes you happy —and same for me. Sofia is gone, so she doesn't have to deal with any of this mess," I said.

"Fine. But I'm not paying for anything," Emilio responded.

Well, I already knew that. He never had money for anything. The lawyer gave us the paperwork a month later. Emilio had told his parents what was happening, and they told him to sue me for alimony. In the state where we lived, if you're married over twelve years, you owe the other person alimony for life.

When he told me he was going to sue me, I told him he was a grown man and needed to fend for himself. This was the whole reason we were getting a divorce—his failure to launch and take care of himself.

"Just get a job and learn how to manage your money," I said.

"No, my parents and brother said you have to pay for me because we were married a long time," Emilio replied.

I didn't understand why they would say something like that. Wouldn't it make more sense to encourage him to be independent or support him themselves? His dad was still a rich doctor in Colombia. His brother was a plastic surgeon in Maine, married to a radiologist, so I knew they had plenty of money.

"You can go ahead and sue me, but I'm not going to pay you anymore. My job is paying for Sofia's college and expenses," I told him. "I'll move to Bolivia or Thailand. I won't work as a doctor, so I'll make no money. And then there will be no money for Sofia. If you want to do that to her, then go ahead and sue me."

He backed down. I was disappointed and angry with Emilio and his family. Things had been pretty civil until money got involved. I couldn't believe they told him to sue me for support. How did they not realize he was a slacker from the beginning?

I know I'm not the only woman who has gone through this. I can count at least six other friends who are physicians with husbands who are just slugs. Maybe it's because, as physicians, we look for partners we can take care of. I'm guessing the common thread is that we all had something happen in childhood that made us feel the need to rescue people. It's a theme in medicine—you help people. Part of it is conscious, but a lot of it is unconscious.

In a way, I thought fighting death and rescuing people was what I needed. I wanted to master what I couldn't do when I was little. But now, after practicing psychiatry for many decades, I know you cannot heal or save everybody.

Some people are too sick or too unwilling to change. Psychiatrists can't fix people alone. All we do is meet and accept people where they are. We can make suggestions or guide them toward change through understanding their pain. But we can't control their actions.

A few days later, my neighbor Josh came back to my door and asked for my phone number. He worked as a pharmaceutical sales rep—the kind of people who push doctors to prescribe certain medications. Those reps are normally attractive people, so you'll listen to what they say. Josh was fit and sexy.

We started texting for a few days, pretty neutral chats—asking about each other's day or just random stuff. Then one day, he texted me out of nowhere:

"Do you shave down there?"

I stared at my phone, shocked. Is that a thing I was supposed to do? We had never talked about anything remotely close to that. I immediately texted my friends and asked if they shaved. I had no idea. I had been living under a rock married to Emilio.

All of my friends said, "Of course we shave. What kind of question is that?" and laughed hysterically at me.

I thought, *Oh shit*, and immediately booked a laser hair removal appointment. I didn't even respond to Josh. I thought, *I'm obviously not ready to play just yet*. I needed to get myself together. And Josh was way off. Who the fuck texts that?!

A few nights later, I heard a knock on the door. It was Josh again. He would always knock at night. I was in my pajamas—and not the cute kind. It was 9 p.m.

"What's up?" I shouted through the door.

"I have an emergency," he said.

I opened the door. "What happened?"

"Oh, nothing. I just wanted to ask for help because I have a wound. I need a doctor to look at me," said Josh.

I examined him, like an idiot, missing his ulterior motive. Looking back, I was a few steps behind him when it came to lust. If I could do it all over again, I'd pick up on the signs—and probably be into it.

So we were sitting together while I looked at his "wound." It was really just a gross pimple. I put some antibiotic cream on it. I wondered if he noticed the bullseye targets hanging all over my walls. I had joined the military and was in a shooting class. I sucked, so I brought home the targets for motivation.

Naturally, the next day I was talking to my friends about what happened. They all said he wanted to sleep with me. I was kind of excited because having a one-night stand was on my bucket list. Not necessarily because I really wanted to, but it seemed like a rite of American passage into adulthood. I had never had that experience. Although I realized having a one-night stand with your neighbor may not be the brightest idea.

A few nights later, he came back with another "emergency."

"What's wrong this time?" I asked.

"I want to have sex with my neighbor," he responded.

"It's too late, and I'm in my PJs. Come back on Friday."

I was excited about sleeping with a hot guy. I really needed to try it—just once—without being in love. Normally, if I'm not madly in love, I can't have sex. But I decided to change my frame of mind. Why not? Time is passing by and I'm no longer a spring chicken.

He came back on Friday at 5p.m., earlier than his normal 9 p.m. knocks.

"Here I am. Are you ready?" said Josh.

"Ready for what?" I asked.

"Ready to have sex."

"Wait," I said. "I at least need some wine. Do you want some wine?"

"No, I'm good."

I poured myself a glass. Then we were just sitting there on the couch. He wasn't talking. The whole scene was strange. I was laughing at how stupid it all was. After about ten minutes, I had another glass or two, a little tipsy now, and I was giving myself a pep talk when he interrupted.

"Should we kiss or what?"

The whole vibe was off. It felt forced and very bizarre, like we were in a scene of a Woody Allen movie.

I sighed. "No, dude. I don't think this is working. I can't do it. Sorry."

He started to walk out, then pointed at the targets on the wall.

"Why do you have those?"

I didn't feel like talking anymore, so I said I would tell him another time.

A week later, he came back with another "emergency." This time, he needed me to lend him $100.

I couldn't believe it—another man just wanting my money. He told me some story about his kid needing the money for a field trip and the school not accepting credit cards.

"Yes, sure. I'll go get it," I said. I gave him the $100. *¿Asi, o mas estúpida?* How can I be so stupid?

Months went by, and I didn't hear from him at all. Then I saw his car get repossessed.

One day, I went over to his house and knocked on the door. "Dude, you know that I'm Colombian, right? Are you really not going to pay me my money back?"

He looked freaked out. I wasn't that upset—mostly just irritated. At myself too. Why would I give him the money in the first place? I had spent so many years giving money to Emilio. It felt good to demand my money back from this fool.

CHAPTER 7

RUNNING UNTIL I COULDN'T

I'VE BEEN small-framed my entire life, hence the nickname *flaca*. Skinny. Part of it was just nature. My parents are both small people, but it was also how busy I kept my body. You can't gain much weight if you are always moving around, and I usually worked two or three jobs at once, staying in motion constantly.

When I ended my marriage, I vowed to start enjoying my time more. I wanted to be healthier without working endless hours. I wanted to have more fun instead of being at the job all the time. So, I started exercising regularly. I even got creative with my fitness and traveled to must-see destinations for hikes. I started learning how to ski, which turned out to be very challenging. I wasn't surprised I was terrible at it despite endless lessons. Part of my mind was always stuck worrying about the multiple ways I could get a skull fracture or a knee injury. But there was something about arriving at the mountain base with no serious injuries; I could prove my mind wrong, which is why I kept trying. I started running too. Maybe it was a midlife crisis, but I knew I just had to keep moving. I was in my mid-forties then, and I'd become hyperaware of aging. Getting old meant inching closer to death. I couldn't lose my mobility because then, I would basically be on my deathbed.

That drive to stay active eventually led me to the military. At the time, life had calmed down a lot. I was working less. Emilio wasn't hanging around, playing his bagpipes so loud I would need a hearing aid before being eligible for social security. Sofia was away in college. The house felt eerily quiet. I had too much free time and was totally alone. Joining felt like a way to fill that void, to stay busy and in an environment I understood.

Being surrounded by guns, chaos, and death felt more familiar than quiet stillness. After years of living in survival mode, the absence of noise felt suffocating in its own way. When you're used to conflict and violence, it's very hard to let it go. You become comfortable in the environments that shape you. I didn't think much about all of that when I signed up—I just wanted to use my skills to help soldiers affected by war. I knew what violence could do to the mind; I had seen it in my family, my friends, my patients, just about everyone I knew.

As expected, the military brought me closer to conflict. I witnessed more suffering, pain, trauma, and death. I saw how war reshaped people, how it messed them up. Looking back, I was so fixated on healing others' traumas because I didn't want to face my own. Helping others felt safer than turning inward, than peeling back the layers of my own pain.

And yet, being in the military gave me something I didn't know I was searching for: a new identity. Without realizing it, I had been longing for the stability that comes with connection. The military brings orphans together and gives you a second family. It offered me belonging, acceptance, and a sense of purpose. I hadn't realized how much I craved that until it was handed to me—uniforms, instructions, customs, and camaraderie filling a void I didn't know was gaping.

At the same time, I threw myself even deeper into my fitness routines. Surrounded by people who woke up early for punishing workouts, I pushed myself to keep up. My body stayed in constant motion.

Then, without warning, my body betrayed me. It started with hip pain—excruciating, unrelenting. After a few weeks of trying to push through, I finally went to my doctor, and he mentioned the possibility of cancer due to an unusual fracture in my hip. He told me I'd need crutches for six months. I was devastated and terrified.

I wasn't ready to die.

There were too many things I wanted to do, too many places I still needed to see. I also feared a drawn-out illness. If I were to die, I hoped it would be a quick end.

The doctor ordered bone scans to check for malignant tumors. Every test came back negative. It wasn't cancer.

A year later, the pain came back. I had several herniated discs in my back. I was happy it wasn't cancer, but it was still awful. I lost the ability to walk and needed crutches for nearly six months again.

Those six months broke me. The pain was unbearable, but worse was the stillness. I couldn't exercise. I couldn't outrun my thoughts. For the first time in my life, I had to sit with them. Depression and anxiety consumed me. I became hyperaware of my mortality. Getting older felt like being trapped in a body that was betraying me, inching closer to death. *Finalmente me cayó la inmunda.* Finally tragedy struck.

This wasn't a new fear—it had been with me since

childhood. Maybe it came from losing my brother, or maybe from growing up surrounded by the constant threat of violence in my native country. From an early age, I understood how fragile life was. I never imagined living to old age. The kind of future where you grow old and have years of quiet, happy retirement never even crossed my mind.

My first brush with death came when I was eight. We were driving on a curvy mountain road to the farm when a tire popped off a truck in front of us. It came barreling toward our car at high speed. There was no room to swerve, nowhere to go. I closed my eyes and pictured the tire smashing into my skull, the sound of metal and glass shattering. Somehow, it missed us by inches, bouncing past like a warning shot.

That moment didn't stand alone. Like most Colombians, I have been cohabitating with misfortune my whole life. Danger was never far away—it lingered like a shadow. It isn't unusual in Colombia for everyone to clap once a plane has landed. Nobody admits it out loud, but we've all been secretly thinking the plane would crash. That unspoken fear shapes how we say goodbye too. When you leave for a big trip, your whole family comes to the airport. They give tearful hugs and long goodbyes, not because they're sentimental, but because there's a real possibility you won't make it back. We Colombians are used to facing death, especially at the hands of others. "*No dejes que te echen tierra.*" Literally, "don't let them bury you." A figure of speech meaning don't let people mistreat you.

Death visited me again when I was ten years old. We were on vacation, and I found myself standing on a tall building terrace, looking down at the street below. I wanted to jump, longing to escape. I wanted to fly, to be free of the heaviness that already pressed on my young mind. In that moment, the ticking clock of life felt too loud, too urgent. I was scared I wouldn't have time to grow up, scared of what the future held. I couldn't imagine a version of my life untouched by illness or death, because it had never existed for me. I decided not to jump, but that feeling of longing to be free stuck with me.

A year later, I tried to join a gymnastics club. I got rejected. The coach told my mom I was too old to start the sport. The rejection devastated me, but I was determined to be a gymnast anyway. I started training on my own, flipping, twisting, and turning across our backyard. I was practicing tumbling one afternoon when I broke my hip. I had to wear a cast for six months. My body felt weak and incapable. I was only eleven and already felt old, fragile, and decrepit. *Una vieja*. An old one.

Ironically, the older I got, the more often I would come face-to-face with illness and death. My childhood self-predicted the future. Near-death experiences clung to me.

Every time I've faced death, I've had vivid visions of what it would be like. In medical school, a homeless man pressed a jagged shard of glass to my belly button. I was just waiting at the bus stop when he approached and threatened me. For a second, I shut my eyes and pictured my body lying flat on an operating table. Surgeons surrounded me while my intestines poured out the side of my body. It didn't end that way. I just gave the guy my jacket and bus fare, and we both went on with our lives. *Me salve de arepa* (a figure of speech meaning a stroke of luck or a very close call).

It's no wonder I went into medicine. If death was going to surround me no matter what, maybe I could at least learn how to outsmart it. From a young age, I was petrified of dying, but at the same time, I seemed to chase after it— drawn to the very thing I feared most. Studying medicine felt like a way to confront that fear head-on or maybe find a cure for every illness that haunted me. Part of me believed I could evade death entirely if I stayed healthy enough, disciplined enough. Like most medical professionals, I take my health seriously. And sometimes, I catch myself feeling untouchable, as if my role as a healer should somehow exempt me from sickness. But deep down, I know that's an illusion. Over the years, I've been relentlessly hard on myself, holding my body to an impossible standard, punishing any sign of weakness as though it were a personal failure.

My fear of death also made me a bit of an obsessive student. In med school, I wasn't just trying to pass my classes—I wanted to master everything. I pored over textbooks until the letters blurred; spent long nights in the anatomy lab memorizing every muscle, nerve, and artery; and volunteered for every extra rotation I could get. I wasn't just ambitious; I was desperate to know the human body inside and out, as if total understanding could give me control over its fragility.

At some point, I bought a human skeleton to help with my studies. I can't remember where or how—maybe from another med student or a random seller—but I do remember the price: $25. It felt like a small investment for the kind of mastery I craved. I named the skeleton Jeronimo. His cranium sat on my bedside table like a silent roommate, a reminder of my mission. The rest of his bones stayed organized in a plastic bag inside my closet, available anytime I needed to review my coursework. Jeronimo became an essential study tool, helping me memorize complex anatomical structures and prepare for exams with the kind of precision I demanded of myself.

Once I finished anatomy, I passed him on to a junior

student. "Promise you'll never sell him," I told her. "Pass him on to a responsible student after you." She just nodded.

I guess I could have taken Jeronimo to a cemetery for a proper burial, but I never thought about that at the time. He wasn't a person to me—he was a tool, a partner in my mission to outsmart death. But he was also someone's son, most likely a victim of poverty and violence who did not get to have a burial. Instead, the body lived in a teenager's closet. *Qué horror*. Sad and horrifying.

Studying medicine still couldn't save me. The next time I thought I was going to die was during my surgical rotation in med school. It was two in the morning, and I was helping in the operating room. We had just finished with a patient, and I had a five-minute break until our next patient came in. I decided to run to the restroom, so I wouldn't be stuck holding it during the entire next surgery. The bathroom door had a faulty lock, so once I went inside, I couldn't come back out.

I was trapped for hours, and I pictured myself dying from asphyxia. *Qué muerte tan pendeja*. What a stupid death. I could imagine my entire body turning blue from lack of oxygen. The bathroom had no windows. The wooden door was too sturdy for me to break, so I sat there, picturing my own death for over two hours until someone found me. The windowless room with the musty and stale air felt like a coffin. When a surgical instrument assistant heard me yelling for help, she flung the door open. I could finally breathe again. I didn't know it at the time, but that experience made me claustrophobic. Small spaces make me feel like I can't breathe.

Later, during my midlife adventures, I attempted scuba diving. The confined space of the mask and being thirty feet under the ocean's surface was awful. Small spaces, planes, even elevators all remind me of that bathroom.

And yet, nothing prepared me for the horror of being sidelined by herniated discs with excruciating pain. Forced to sit still, I felt like I was dying over and over again. I started having panic attacks all the time. I relived my traumas on repeat in my mind. It was like I had opened a wound in my mind, and it was bleeding profusely. Nothing would stop the flood of memories and pain. I couldn't sleep. I lost my appetite. I felt powerless. Every time a friend brought me medicine or food, I felt like a terrible burden on them, on everyone. Eventually, I isolated myself. I hated needing help from others. Feeling alone and trapped, I had nothing to do but sit there while my heart raced uncontrollably.

Memories of past brushes with death consumed all my thoughts. Like the time I had a bad reaction to a medication and developed an arrhythmia. My heart would beat fast and irregularly. It felt like it was doing somersaults up my throat and trying to escape through my mouth. I was in the emergency room one night, waiting for tests back, when I saw the monitor near my bed show that my heart rate was over 250 beats per minute.

I panicked, positive I was going to code. I called the nurse, halfway passed out. I started praying and making promises to God to be a better person, even though I was proud to be an atheist until that day. When I saw the heart monitor, and my certain demise, I clung back to Jesus. *¡Dios mío! ¡Ayúdame!* Good God, help me! I promise to be good!

The nurse ran in and explained that I wasn't looking at my heart rate, but my neighbor's. I was fine. I felt stupid and embarrassed. *Qué vergüenza.* Shameful. My fear of that deathly threshold had made it feel real and immediate.

The inevitability of death ran through my mind like an endless reel while I waited for my discs to heal, with no way to escape the weight of my thoughts. Worries and guilt consumed me so completely it was hard to breathe. I no longer enjoyed life. Nothing made me smile anymore. My mind was cruel, replaying every mistake I had ever made. I thought about the times I was impatient or mean to my sisters, the countless ways I could have been more present for my mother.

I couldn't stop reliving the day I begged her to take me to buy those red shoes, the day my baby brother died. The guilt wrapped around me. I kept thinking about how his death was my fault. My thoughts turned to Sofia, to the times I punished her for yelling or being emotional as a child, not realizing how much I was carrying out the behavior of my parents and grandparents. And then there was my career—I had become a doctor, dedicating my life to healing others, yet I still couldn't save my own mother or the children from the jungle. That failure, too, cut deep. It felt like proof that I had fallen short in every role: sister, daughter, mother, wife, healer.

I felt nothing but failure.

Before my injury, I had been adventurous, chasing after exciting trips and fun. Of course, those also led to close encounters with death. The sixth time I thought I was going to die happened while I was on vacation in Southeast Asia. I caught a dreadful virus and spent three weeks in the hospital in Hanoi. My lungs were filled with fluid, and I lost twenty pounds. Every breath felt like I was wheezing. I had severe anemia and became delirious and septic. When I was finally able to fly back home, I had to spend another week in the hospital in isolation. It took my body months to recover. I prepared my end-of-life documents, again certain it was the end. Since then, I've always got my will and other documents ready to go, just in case.

When I finally returned to work at the prison, a guard that moonlighted as a priest after hours, approached me and anointed me with blessed oil. He said he could see death clinging to me.

He was right. It didn't stop. One day, I noticed a tiny pimple on my scalp. I kept an eye on it for a few weeks, rubbing across it every time I'd wash my hair. It bled a little. I made an appointment with my dermatologist. I assumed it was cancerous, and it was. The mass was under the skin and extended seven inches long and one inch deep. It looked like a small pimple on the surface, but I knew it was worse before the doctor even told me. The doctor explained that if the mass were to touch the bone, I would need radiotherapy. Thankfully, he was able to remove the mass. I sat crying while I waited for the on-site biopsy report.

"This is the type of cancer you would like to have," he told me. *El muy hijueputa.* Fucking son of a bitch. "Some of them travel fast, and you die within a year. At least we know this isn't that."

I was angry that he had no compassion for how panicked I was. The biopsy showed that the mass was indeed cancerous. I had it removed. Every time I wash my hair, I still check my scalp for weird pimples and bumps.

Each of those near-death experiences stayed with me, lingering in the back of my mind like unfinished business. That's why I just kept moving—*pate perro* for life. Staying busy had always been my way of outrunning the memories, of keeping the fear at bay. But once I was stuck on those crutches, it all caught up to me. Sitting on my couch all day felt eerily similar to being trapped in that med school bathroom, counting every breath and wondering if it would be my last. Even the act of trying to hobble from one room to another left me feeling weak and frail, like I was reliving my fright, all over again. Every small struggle became a reminder that death was still nearby, waiting patiently. Plus I lived alone. What if I choked on a piece of potato and there was no one around to do the Heimlich or call 911? I had researched Life Alert for *abuelitos*, grandparents, and motorized wheelchairs, but I refused to buy one of those just yet.

It took me almost four months before I finally asked for professional help. I had reached my limit. I was stuck on crutches and could not let the emotional pain paralyze me.

CHAPTER 8

UNATTACHED

UP UNTIL MY INJURY, I spent most of my time taking care of others. It was second nature. I did it at home with Emilio and Sofia, both while we lived together and after. I did it every day at work. Even as a child, I was a caretaker. My younger sister was neglected by our parents, so she latched onto me. She was three, and I was only eight, but I was the only one available.

I endured pressures like an adult, responsible for my sister, for watching over my mother, and for maintaining perfect grades at school. I felt like I skipped childhood and learned that life was painful and unfair. I was made hyper-aware of how hard illness and death could be. Adults treated me like one of them. I saw children as silly, dependent, and annoying, especially my sister. I could never enjoy the few moments of respite I got because I was too busy anticipating the tragedies around the corner. I hated my house, my city, my school. I still do.

I grew up in a cold and violent home that left me feeling trapped and numb. But I was also just a child. I did not know how to express these feelings; I didn't have the words.

And my parents did not set a good example of how to handle emotions. I knew what was happening, I could feel it, but I couldn't express it appropriately. I buried a lot of feelings and moved forward as if nothing was wrong. It's what I knew how to do.

I never dealt with or processed the resentment I carried for my father and his relentless abuse of my mother; I simply wished he was dead. I wished my mother could be someone else—someone more capable, someone who could take care of us. I pushed my middle sister away emotionally and bullied her, not because I didn't care, but because I was overwhelmed. Being in charge was the only thing I knew.

That pattern followed me into adulthood. After my divorce, I realized that Emilio was an extension of my childhood—he was just another example of the same pattern, another person I took care of while ignoring my own needs. My only comfort was being in control. It was how I managed the chaos, the uncertainty, and the anxiety that had been with me for a long time.

I took that obsessive control into motherhood too. It wasn't until recently that I realized I was also an overcontrolling parent. I was never violent, but my parenting style was dominant. I expected a lot from Sofia, especially when it came to discipline and behavior. Without even thinking, I had started using some of the same methods my grandparents used on me to keep her quiet as a child.

One of those methods was the *el juego del silencio*, the silence game, something I learned directly from my grandmother. We played it often on road trips. Everyone in the car had to stop talking, and the first person to speak would be punished—usually with chores like washing dishes for the rest of the trip. It was framed as a game, but the message was clear: Silence was the goal, and obedience was the standard.

When we took trips with Sofia, I did the exact same thing.

Last time I visited Sofia, we were sitting at a nice restaurant when a nearby child started acting out—yelling, hitting, completely out of control. Sofia laughed and said, "Sounds like it's time for *el juego del silencio*." Her words hit me hard. I was mortified. In that moment, I realized I had passed down the very same silencing tactics that messed me up as a kid.

That moment forced me to reflect on what I had normalized—not just in parenting, but in how I handled emotions and control. I realized that by enforcing silence, Sofia grew to be very shy and reserved. She is not comfortable speaking up.

Sofia is doing psychoanalytic therapy now. At first, I questioned it. I reminded her that she had a good childhood and asked what she even talked to the therapist about. I wasn't dismissive, but I was confused. She told me she found it helpful. She was working on being more assertive and calmer.

The silencing didn't start with me, but it didn't end with me either. I thought of that horrible Catholic elementary school run by German nuns, where silence was enforced and fear was routine. The rules were rigid and the discipline was harsh. There was no love, no compassion. My kindergarten teacher, Ms. Irene, would pull our earlobes and arms if we didn't follow instructions. The nuns made me clean the toilet if I needed to use the restroom, so I started avoiding it. Decades later, my bladder still pays the price for holding in urine for ten hours at a time.

There was no space for fun. Even the school bus was

silent. I adapted by staying quiet and doing everything perfectly. The lessons I learned about control, silence, and self-denial stayed with me much longer than any report card.

The generational trauma didn't start with me. It didn't even start with my parents. These patterns—silence, survival, escape—go back further. They were passed down and shaped by circumstances that none of us chose.

When my dad was seven years old, he saw people murdered with machetes in the countryside. He had to run and hide from bandits as a small child, learning early on that survival meant staying quiet and disappearing when necessary.

I don't like to associate with people who are attention-seeking or demand a spotlight on them. It is in my genes. The more invisible you are, the better it goes for you. If people notice you, they will take advantage of you. My dad understood that from a young age, and I did too.

At home, things were no better for my dad. His mother beat him so badly he would flee to the neighbors' house for safety. Sometimes he would hop on a local train and live there for days, selling sweets to passengers and probably surviving on those sweets as well.

Those habits didn't disappear. They shifted. From Sofia's childhood obsession with chocolate to my continued purchasing of *bocadillo veleño* (a sweet treat made with guava paste; a common rhyme says *"bocadillo veleño que quita el hambre y quita el sueño,"* the sweet snack will stop you from being hungry or sleepy), we carry more than we realize. The coping mechanisms—eating sweets, escaping to avoid pain and discomfort, staying silent to stay safe—are learned behaviors passed down from generation to generation. From my dad's upbringing, then my grandfather fleeing the Holocaust, it was passed down from both sides. I had a double dose of *pate perro*. It's all a pattern laid like a recurring tile mosaic in our psyche. We may each live our lives differently, but the instincts are the same. We run. We hide. We look for comfort wherever we can find it.

Thankfully, Sofia is more well-balanced and healthier than me. She says she's grateful her parents were opposites —for every way that I was overcontrolling, Emilio was chill to a fault. During her childhood, Sofia was an overachiever like me. She did ballet and ice skating. She had perfect grades (except for physics). Some days, she would have skating practice from 5 to 7 a.m., then go to school, then go on to after-school programs from 5 to 8 p.m. Busy was her default. Once she was an adult, she thanked me for her sense of discipline.

With Sofia away at college, Emilio out of the house, and my body forcing me to rest, I started to reflect more honestly on how deeply I had carried those early cycles from my childhood into adulthood. As a child, I learned to be rigid and emotionally closed off while still being the one expected to care for everyone else. When I met Emilio, I unknowingly repeated the same dynamic. He was extremely passive and easygoing, and he had no problem letting me take the lead on everything. From the beginning, he decided to step back and let the load fall entirely on my shoulders—without ever asking if I was okay with that. It was like taking care of my mother and sister all over again.

After my baby brother died, I developed the belief that bad things happen when people aren't being watched closely enough. Nobody had been paying attention to him; nobody anticipated what could go wrong. That loss never left me. I always felt like I had to be attentive and cater to those in need. So when Emilio started to show me that he was not really a partner, I didn't view him as a grown man failing to step up. I saw someone fragile. I saw someone who needed protection. He became another helpless child in my care, and I didn't want another tragedy on my watch.

He had sweet moments—like when he brought home the cat for Sofia—but he was also incredibly irresponsible. He moved through life like a teenager without a plan. He lost jobs. He missed appointments. He left messes for others to clean up. I provided everything for him. I wasn't just his wife. I was his mother.

It makes me think about how my grandad would call my grandma *"mama"* as an endearing term. And how I call Sofia *"mama"* at times too. *Qué cosa tan rara.* Weird, messed up.

I stayed with Emilio for eighteen years because, in many ways, the relationship felt familiar. It didn't occur to me that my idea of "normal" was rooted in old patterns. I convinced myself that things were fine because I was holding every-thing together. That illusion of stability made it easier to stay, even when I was exhausted.

Eventually, I recognized the pattern. I thought, I'm getting sucked into this again and it's too much. I need to get out. But breaking free wasn't simple. I was just on autopilot, repeating the pattern. While Emilio enjoyed life, biking, swimming, going out for smoothies, I was the idiot working all the time. I kept thinking it had to stop. It took almost two decades, but I got to a point where I realized that no matter what I did, things were going to continue the same. It is hard for anyone to change, and almost impossible for some.

Emilio represents the first type of man that I was attracted to: handsome, harmless, and passive. Men like that are also looking for a mother figure to guide them. When Emilio and I split up, I went for the exact opposite.

The other category of men I've dated are hot, athletic, and aggressive. They were each military men, with an extra edge of being ex-special forces operatives.

They were also assholes—emotionally unavailable, egotistical, and even misogynistic. I didn't make the connection at first. One day Sofia, always blunt, asked me why I was giving chances to "undeserving wife beaters." It made me step back. The resemblance to my dad was hard to ignore.

My father's joking about his affairs, even naming my younger sister after his mistress like it was no big deal, normalized this kind of cruel behavior in my home for years. The lesson stayed with me—men were allowed to be assholes.

After Emilio, I ended up dating men who carried the same traits, the same inclinations, if not the same violence, as my father. They treated vulnerability like weakness. One of them called me a "pussy" once because I could not pass the scuba diving test due to my claustrophobia. But I kept returning to them.

At the time, I didn't question it. I would meet someone attractive and go for it. I didn't stop to ask, why this person? I wasn't focusing on my patterns. It took repeating the same dynamic over and over for me to even realize there was a pattern.

One of those men was Ryan, a former special forces guy. We first met at the community pool near my house. For a while, we just made small talk there—nothing more. Then one day when I left home to go to my car, I found a message from him inside a used, squished water bottle on the windshield. The paper said, "This is Ryan, the pool guy. Call me," and listed his phone number. I smiled. It was nice to feel that a hot guy was interested in me.

I didn't think about how he knew where I lived or how he knew what car I drove. I thought the whole mystery surrounding the delivery of the message was rather romantic. Only later did I find out he had tracked me down using some sort of satellite system when I walked back from the pool to my house. He never asked for my number, but he knew where I lived. Most people would probably call that creepy, maybe even unhinged, and definitely a red flag. But I was excited. This man seemed daring and audacious. A total 180 from what I had dealt with being married to Emilio.

Ryan lived in a nearly empty house covered in surveillance cameras. The walls were all white with no decorations, no signs of life. The only exception was his bedroom. It was completely blacked out with thick padded walls, no windows, and a single image of a dark night with a full moon taped to the ceiling. He didn't have a bed; he would sleep on the floor over a tatami. He kept ammunition under his pillow and hidden in the ceiling. He spent his days enslaved to rigid exercise routines and set mealtimes and menus. His nights were spent like he was still in the middle of the jungle, sleeping on the ground and looking at the sky. Any variation in his day would upset him. He had constant nightmares in his sleep. I told myself he had been shaped by war.

By now, I realize I should have run. He was a very angry and controlling man, just like my dad. I brushed off things that most people would find deeply concerning. Like the time he FaceTimed me while he was shitting in a toilet and smoking. It's not that I didn't see the warning signs: I just didn't register them as warnings. Instead, they felt familiar, even reassuring. His intensity felt normal. His control felt like care. His disrespect was ubiquitous. That was the framework I'd learned—and I didn't challenge it until much later. You would think, why is this *pendeja* (stupid woman) in love with this asshole? The simple answer was that, whatever unresolved childhood issues I had, lingered. I kept trying to master life and navigate past them without even realizing I was putting myself in the same situations over and over again.

Ryan wasn't the only man I fell for who lacked empathy. There were others—shorter flings with men whose chaotic childhoods had left them emotionally stunted. Many had serious anger issues and were deeply dysfunctional. The pattern stayed the same, dug itself in even deeper with each repetition.

One of them lived in a room that looked like a bunker. Everything was military grade. The furniture, the curtains, even the decor—it was all camouflage or some shade of green. Grenades sat openly on the shelves, next to a book titled *The Art of Manipulation*. He didn't try to hide anything. He also had several women on his roster. I was just one of many on his rotating schedule.

He was one of the men who, at some point, turned to me and asked for a diagnosis—as if I could write him a prescription to fix asshole. Those men were trouble. But the experience wasn't all negative. It was nice to have sexual attention. And I know that what I went through with them is what allowed me to see the pattern. They were a necessary step in my journey so that I could become aware of the patterns. I was either drawn to meek and needy guys or just the opposite—aggressive and on edge. I was either in control of them or completely controlled by them. Two sides of a dysfunctional coin.

Even as I cycled through these relationships, I still told

myself I was doing fine—functioning, capable, and dating hot younger guys. I was doing great!

Being aware of the patterns does not prevent me from falling for the same. My deep childhood scars continuously draw me towards violence. I enjoy violent movies. I like working in aggressive environments with the military, with the mentally ill, or with inmates; I gravitate toward it.

My wounds do not bleed anymore, but the scars have left some dents. I get anxious in crowded places. I get easily startled by loud noises. I have nightmares. I fear death and hate funerals. I am a worrywart and a total fatalist. I tend to care for others to excess. I am attracted to certain kinds of men. All my choices had been colored by trauma.

After my injury and being unable to run my thoughts away, I began to think about identity and legacy. I wished I could drop my father's last name and take my mother's instead. That change would feel like a better reflection of who I am, and a way to honor her and my grandfather.

I've also thought about cutting ties with my native country, but as long as my parents are alive, I don't see that as a real option. So I remain connected—to them and to the history that shaped me.

People often assume that being a psychiatrist must be emotionally difficult. For me, it is not. Once I learned as a child that I had to build an emotional wall around me and, once the wall was in place, I operated without much reaction. I didn't get overwhelmed. I didn't emotionally absorb what my patients were going through because I didn't emotionally absorb anything. I've seen patients cut their wrists with plastic utensils while hospitalized. I stayed calm. One patient walked into a lake and never came back. I didn't react when I learned what happened. It wasn't detachment or neglect—I still did my job. But I did it from behind a barrier. Focusing on other people's pain was easier than addressing my own. In a strange way, it made the work more manageable.

Even the most extreme cases rarely got to me. My patients didn't shake me—not the one who put part of his bloody earlobe in a letter or the one who castrated himself with a soda can. I had many more who swallowed razor blades or who swallowed screws. Some smeared feces or blood on the walls. One ate his own semen; another ate his poop. I stayed steady through all of it.

There was the woman who cut open her nine-year-old son with a knife. Another woman strangled her sister, claiming she was following God's whispers. Neither of them unnerved me. I've worked with a child who was the lone survivor of a house fire that killed his entire family, and with a Catholic bishop who had several nuns as lovers. *Ave Maria.* I remember the details, not the emotion.

I've often wondered if my background—my exposure to violence, my early understanding of survival—made me unusually fit for psychiatry. I can stay present in the face of chaos. I can keep my focus, keep my role, when everything around me breaks apart. It's not that I don't feel. I just focus on how to fix the presenting problem. I think about how I can be helpful and how I can decrease suffering. That ability was necessary, and in many ways, it still is.

CHAPTER 9

THE DOCTOR BECOMES THE PATIENT

ONCE I STARTED TRAINING in psychiatry, I spent a lot of time reflecting on how early traumas quietly control your entire life—your relationships, your reactions, your career. It's all connected. Trauma becomes the invisible hand guiding your choices, often without your permission or even awareness. I understood the theories inside and out. I could explain them in a lecture, spot them in a patient, and write a treatment plan. But acknowledging how those same theories applied to me was a different story.

Part of me—the part that was used to being a clinician—recognized every red flag. I knew I had unresolved issues like getting upset when I felt someone was taking advantage of me, even if they weren't. I had treated similar issues in others, but I couldn't get out of their hold over me. I had convinced myself that I did not have time to waste dwelling on the past. I knew it would break me if I were to talk about all the pain I had safely stored away. I refused to do it. That is, not until I was injured and trapped on my couch, physically grounded and mentally spiraling.

Movement was my medicine. Running, lifting, hiking,

skiing, working—anything to stay ahead of the trauma, the pain. So when I got injured, stillness hit me like a freight train. With nothing to distract me, the anxiety came flooding in. The depression was relentless. I couldn't outpace it anymore. After a few months, I reached out to a therapist.

I'd always recommended therapy to others, told people it was a powerful tool for healing, that it could change their lives. Somehow, I never thought I needed it myself. I thought I was built differently. My injury challenged that belief.

The pain was getting worse by the day. The doctor gave me steroid pills, hoping they would ease it, which they did, but they also worsened my anxiety and depression. Meanwhile, I was miserable, even on the days when the pain had eased. Isolated and injured, I started having frequent anxiety attacks. My heart would race, my chest would tighten, and I would feel dizzy and nauseous. I was convinced my blood pressure was sky-high or that my old arrhythmia had returned. One night, I was so sure I was about to pass out that I called my neighbor in a panic, just so someone would know if I dropped dead in my living room.

"I don't want to go to the ER because they're going to do too many tests. I'll be stuck there for hours," I explained.

"So what do you want me to do?" they asked.

"Take me to the fire station, please. They have an EKG machine. I just have to make sure my heart is okay."

When we got to the fire station, there was just one female firefighter there. She stared at me up and down but never examined me.

"Ma'am, are you anxious?" she asked.

I was insulted. I thought, what the fuck. Of course I am anxious, I have an arrhythmia.

"No. Something is wrong. I had an arrhythmia before, and now my heart is beating out of whack," I told her.

She did an EKG and there was no arrhythmia. I started searching Google for a therapist that night.

Three months later, when I finally showed up to my first appointment, the first thing I said was, "The fact that I'm here is terrible. This is not okay. I can't believe I'm starting therapy."

I meant it. Sitting on that video call felt like defeat, like I'd lost control. It was during the COVID years, when everything felt apocalyptic and surreal. I was terrified of the virus. So I stayed inside, even when I was physically able to leave. Those years forced everyone into stillness, and for someone like me, that was torture.

It took a global pandemic, an injury, and a body that refused to cooperate to make me pause. For the first time in my life, I wasn't moving. *Pate perro* no more. I wasn't helping anyone else. I was just sitting in the wreckage, surrounded by years of trauma that had finally caught up to me. I couldn't outrun it this time. I had always coped by staying busy, by doing—but now there was nothing left to do but feel.

I needed to get out. But I couldn't do it alone.

My therapist was a blond, Western European woman in her forties. All I could see on the web camera background was her light blue couch and some fresh flowers sitting on a table. As soon as we started in earnest, I lost it. I cried nonstop. She was just sitting there, and I thought about how I was wasting the session. I couldn't pull it together either. I had no control over my tears. They just poured out.

I normally never cried. If someone insulted me, I didn't cry. If I hurt myself, no tears. I just put on my strong face and kept doing what I had to do, even as a child.

The therapist didn't even have to ask a question—just being in that appointment, acknowledging I needed help, and sitting with that level of vulnerability was too much. I started crying immediately. I wasn't in control. And up until then, I had convinced myself I had everything handled. My logic had always been: If I worry enough, plan enough, stay ahead of the worst-case scenarios, then nothing can touch me. But I was clearly unraveling.

By our third session, I managed to stop sobbing long enough to talk—barely. I tried to explain what had happened, all the things piling up in my mind. I got a few sentences out before the tears came back.

"Just concentrate on the present. Pay attention to your feelings, thoughts, and surroundings in a nonjudgmental manner," she told me.

It sounded straightforward, but it wasn't. I had spent my whole life trying to fix things. Solve problems. So once all my old pain bubbled up, I felt responsible for resolving it. All of it. Every single incident, mistake, regret—I thought I had to work through it all at once. I was sinking. My mind was running wild with anxiety, and there was no way out.

"Start writing," she said. "Everything. All of your memories. Let it out. You have to cry it out."

It felt like I had spent my entire life stacking lids over everything that had ever happened to me. Every time something painful came up, I didn't process it—I just sealed it off and kept moving. One lid over childhood abuse at the hands of my father and educators. *Las malditas monjas.* Those damn nuns. Another over the death of my baby brother. Another over my mother's mental illness. Another over the struggle of my marriage. Another over the divorce. I just kept covering it up, one layer at a time, thinking I was managing it. But over the years, those layers got heavier. Eventually, the weight of it all became unbearable. I was crumbling under something I had built myself.

When the therapist told me to start journaling, I dismissed it. I didn't think it was for me. I never understood the point of writing things down—what was I supposed to do, cry into a notebook and suddenly feel better? It sounded useless. I was used to solving problems, not feeling them. Writing felt like stalling. But I had tried everything else, and nothing was working.

"Go to the park," the therapist said. "Observe the lake, the currents, the trees from different angles. Feel the sun and the wind. Let yourself be present. Then write."

I didn't think it would work, but I had nothing else to do. So one morning, I grabbed my crutches and hobbled across the street. The park was small, quiet. The lake was surrounded by tall trees, with just a few scattered houses in the distance. Ducks floated aimlessly. Birds chirped, squirrels darted through the grass. Occasionally, I would spot an alligator.

There was only one bench—shaded under a big tree. I lowered myself onto it carefully. I couldn't go any farther. My back and hip pain made everything feel impossible. So I sat. I watched the water move with the breeze. I tried to breathe. I stared at the empty page in my notebook.

It took me a long time to even decide which language to use—Spanish or English. Neither felt quite right. But eventually, after watching the lake and the animals for what felt like hours, I started to write. Just incident by incident, whatever came to mind. I barely got through a sentence before the tears started again. Every word pulled up a memory. Going to the park became my new routine. I had a new purpose. I needed to heal inside and out.

I cried until I didn't have any tears left. But I kept writing.

Eventually, I sat down and read through what I had written. I was looking for a pattern—some thread that could explain it all. I knew it had to be there. I had felt it for years, just under the surface. What I didn't expect was how obvious it would be once I saw it in writing. Page after page, the same themes repeated: violence, loss, and death. Over and over. I had normalized it. I had lived with it. I had run from it and then turned around and ran straight back into it.

That realization felt like a second awakening. These weren't isolated memories—they were a pattern I had been unconsciously choosing. I didn't just survive violence. I surrounded myself with it. I moved toward it. It was like choosing to live on a military base in the middle of a war zone, again and again. At twenty-two, I didn't realize it, but I kept returning to what was familiar, even if it hurt. Even marrying Emilio—a pilot—was its own kind of repetition. I had been holding on to the image of those model airplanes flying over my baby brother's grave. Without knowing it, I was reenacting my own pain, over and over. My choices kept me locked in the same cycle.

Walking to the lake to write and cry became my new habit. It was healing. My therapist was helping me break free of what was sinking me. My thoughts and my memories, they had become a mesh net that was tangled around me. It was dragging me down when I couldn't untangle it. I had held onto my trauma, trapped it under so many lids, across decades.

A friend once shared a metaphor for trauma that stuck with me. Imagine holding an empty cup—it's light, easy to carry. At first, you barely notice it in your hand. But then, little by little, you keep adding water. The cup doesn't change shape, but it gets heavier. At some point, it becomes hard to hold. Not because the cup itself changed, but because of everything it's holding. That's what trauma felt like for me. I had been carrying a full cup for years, pretending it was still light. I finally realized I needed to pour it out. My arm was tired. My whole body was tired. I couldn't keep holding it like that.

Starting therapy was a good decision—one I probably should have made sooner. It helped me identify the patterns at the root of everything I'd been carrying. I was stuck, and my therapist gave me a way out: nature. She told me to go outside, to pay attention to what was happening at the moment. The ducks, the squirrels, the wind in the trees—none of them gave a fuck about my pain. They were just living. And slowly, I was learning to do the same. I was gaining awareness, and I was accepting who I was without criticism.

"Okay, you got it all out," she told me one day. "Now you need to start writing the good stuff. Write what you are grateful about. Go see the birds. Write about nature."

Writing during those quiet moments by the lake helped me reconnect with the world around me. Watching the water move reminded me that time was still passing. Seasons were changing. Life was happening, even if I felt frozen. I began to accept my anxiety instead of constantly trying to control it. I didn't need to fix everything. I just needed to be present.

Once grief stopped overwhelming me, I had the space to process more. I wasn't the doctor anymore—I was finally the patient.

I was surprised. I think that all doctors, whether we realize it or not, think we are immune to sickness because we are high functioning. You have to perform and take care of patients at some of the most stressful times in your life and theirs. There isn't space to get caught up in emotions. Being a doctor doesn't make you immune, even when it feels like you should be the one who knows the answers. You are the one who must have their shit together, who takes care of people at their worst. That's probably why most doctors never disclose that they are sick, impaired, or depressed. Doctors avoid treatment. When you're a doctor, your identity is all about helping other people. So if you need help yourself, your entire identity is gone.

I started that pattern of always being the caretaker, never asking for care, very young. I finished medical school when I was twenty-one. I was young and quickly embraced putting up the facade that everything was fine. I couldn't acknowledge my scars; I was healing other people's. I never had time to slow down and think about what was happening inside of me. I threw myself into understanding what was happening to others. I had been immersed in understanding my patients and their problems. Emilio and his problems. My mother, my father, my sisters—everyone in my life.

In a way, I had spent most of my adult life trying to master what I could not as a child: heal the ill, prevent people from dying, control the aggressor, make the unavailable loved one available. I realized I had been trying to achieve the impossible my entire life. I was also trying to avoid confronting my long-standing fears and core beliefs about safety and trust. Damn, it was a lot at once.

One day, a close friend from medical school called to check on me. He was an intern when I was a med student. I told him that I had started seeing a therapist for overwhelming anxiety. I expected him to be surprised to hear that I had anxiety now.

"You've had anxiety attacks since I've known you," he responded.

I blinked, surprised. He reminded me of a time when I was eighteen and he was working at the hospital. I had made my dad rush me to the ER because I was having chest pain. Apparently, I had demanded to see the cardiologist, certain I was dying. I have no memory of that day.

"I saw you, and there was nothing wrong with your heart. It was an anxiety attack," he said.

Nobody had told me that, but I would have been offended or refused to believe them. But apparently my chest pains were not new; I'd had them since I was eighteen. Probably even before that.

Therapy was a worthwhile investment. I made real progress, uncovering parts of myself with the guidance of my therapist. I started learning to accept my flaws, be grateful, and practice forgiveness—not just toward others but toward myself. I knew there were people I needed to apologize to. My sisters were first. Facing those conversations was intimidating. It forced me to confront mistakes I had long pushed aside. But I knew it was necessary if I wanted to move forward.

My middle sister didn't accept my apology. I had let my younger sisters down many times, especially her. She was born after Javiercito died—a replacement baby. Our parents never spoke of Javiercito, and that silence affected all of us. When my sister arrived, I kept my distance, afraid of losing another baby sibling. I avoided closeness because I didn't know how to handle that kind of pain. Meanwhile, our parents also failed her, and she tried to latch on to me. But I couldn't give her what she needed. I was cold and distant most of our childhood.

I let her down again when Emilio and I moved to the

United States. My sisters had been excited to help with Sofia's arrival, but I took her away and left them behind with our parents. They felt abandoned. I had to accept that my relationship with my sister was broken, shaped by the traumas we all carried. It was painful, but it was also honest. Accepting that was the first step toward healing—even if the path forward wasn't clear yet.

When my therapist first suggested I try to repair my relationships with my parents and sisters, I thought it was impossible. Still, I was willing to try. It took me six months just to make that first phone call—to start talking about the past. No one was really ready for those conversations. Everyone was still burying their own pain, holding on to their own shit.

I tried to make peace with my dad too. One day, he told me he was proud of his daughters.

"You do realize we're just lucky, right?" I said. "We could have ended up completely messed up, given the childhood we had—filled with cheating, beatings, and lies."

He exploded. Denial took over him completely.

"What are you talking about, Ana?" he yelled. He always calls me Ana, even though everyone else calls me Dolores.

I told him to forget it. The conversation wasn't worth my time. Just months earlier, he'd gotten into an argument with my youngest sister and struck her. I wasn't ready to face his anger again.

My middle sister refuses to forgive me, yet she gives our abusive father a pass. She does not even acknowledge there was abuse and violence during our younger years. Complete denial.

"What abuse?" she would say. "I do not know what you are talking about."

I also reached out to my youngest sister. She was more open. As part of her midlife crisis, she changed her career from engineering to cultural astronomy. She talks about the moon's influence on women's cycles and how cosmic understanding shapes human life. She tries to interpret the relationship between tribes and the cosmos. I believe this is an attempt to find meaning and perhaps surrender control to a higher power. This is her way of dealing with the past. I'm grateful she keeps the lines of communication open. That small connection means a lot, even if the rest remains complicated.

Before my injury, I traveled a lot for work. During my trips, I would often find myself randomly in front of a cemetery. I wouldn't seek them out. For five straight years, random wrong turns or getting on the wrong bus would lead me straight to a cemetery in these new cities. It felt strange —like these encounters with the dead were more than coincidence. There was something meaningful hidden beneath it all, though I couldn't quite grasp what.

Around two years before I got injured, I was on a work trip and came across yet another cemetery. After that, I decided to attend a Santería ceremony close to where I lived. At that point, I thought, why not? It sounded like the dead were trying to contact me. The priestess was dressed entirely in white. There were roosters milling about on the patio. The setting was intimate and quiet.

We didn't exchange names or stories. Instead, the priestess told me a woman wearing a black habit with a black veil and white *serre-tête* was watching over me. She had a big smile. The woman she described sounded exactly like Mother Maria Rose, the only nun who was fun and sweet to me in school. She described my grandfather too and even called him by his Austrian name. Over and over, she reassured me that I was being cared for—that I was not alone.

I left feeling overwhelmed. I drove home in a daze and even missed the highway exit to my home. *Brujería*, witchcraft, I thought, stunned and reeling from the experience. I never went back, but that moment stayed with me. I even tried Santería before therapy. Go figure. The stigma of mental health issues and treatment is unquestionable. Like my sister, I was looking for answers in occult powers, digging for answers anywhere but where they actually lay.

Therapy helped me understand what I could fix and what I couldn't. All my shit was out now—laid in front of me in the journal. I couldn't run from it. I couldn't pretend it didn't exist. I had to accept it. Attempting those conversations with my family provided a lot of relief. It decreased my emotional load because I at least tried to apologize for my mistakes. I didn't want to hang on to the emotions anymore. If you don't fix things with people while they are alive, then when they die, you get screwed over with a bunch of unresolved grief. Repairing these relationships is a slow, fragile process filled with setbacks and small victories. But I'm learning that some bridges take time to rebuild, and sometimes the hardest part is just showing up.

Years later, I visited a Buddhist monastery. The monks talked about how life is always changing, how you can't hold on or control it. Religion never gave me peace. Catholic school had taught me obedience, not comfort. The nuns were strict, teaching us to sit still, mind our manners, do our work, and keep quiet. I still can't shake that behavior. I fear God like any good Catholic, but believing feels impossible. It's insane when you think about it—how dare I reject both fathers: the violent one I have on Earth and the punisher in heaven? I tried other religions, too, searching for answers, but Buddhism was the only one that made some sense to me.

The monastery I visited sat high on Mount Koja in Japan. It was freezing cold up there. The monks asked us all the same question: How should you live? Their answer was simple. Let go. Stop clinging to life like it's something you can own. Suffering, they said, comes from holding on in a world that's always moving.

I remember the garden there too. Wild and overgrown, weeds and flowers tangled together. The monks said it reflected the universe—and our messy minds. From one angle it looked like chaos; from another, beauty. That's life, they said. Shift your view and everything changes.

"It's a call to let life happen," one monk told me. "Control is just an illusion."

I nodded like I understood, but my mind kept drifting to my life in Colombia and the early years in America, all those days in the Bronx when I felt crushed by the chaos. Back then, I thought medicine was only about fixing bodies —stopping the bleed, curing the infection, holding the line. But sitting there, years later, I realized it's about whole people. They're big, messy ecosystems, like that garden. You can't untangle the weeds from the flowers. You have to figure out how to support the whole ensemble.

Even in the Bronx, when I didn't have these words to describe it, part of me just knew there was a better way for me to practice medicine. I wanted to be able to support patients, not just with isolated symptoms, but with their whole lives and all the chaos. Would my experience have been different in the Bronx if I'd known how to let go of control? To embrace the chaos? Probably. Perhaps I would have enjoyed it.

CHAPTER 10

FULL CIRCLE

I INVITED my younger sister on a trip to celebrate my fifty-third birthday. It was never my plan, but I was hoping to meet Sofia in Switzerland to have some much-needed mother–daughter time. When Sofia suggested that I invite my sisters and their kids, it seemed like a good idea. I don't normally celebrate my birthday—I've hated parties since the day Javiercito died. I can still see the house lit up, cars pouring down the driveway. I expected to walk into the smell of great food, the sound of laughter and music, but I was met with the sudden absence of my baby brother. That terrible day—and being so wrong about what was happening—ruined parties for me forever.

But I did want to keep working on my relationship with my sisters, so I invited them to celebrate my birthday with me. It wasn't just a trip—it felt like an investment in repairing what time, distance, and old wounds had frayed. It was expensive: an all-inclusive resort and tons of ski time (and with only ten days to plan, the flights were expensive as hell too). Still, it felt worth it. I knew my job paid better than both of my sisters', so I didn't mind footing the bill if it meant we'd have the space and comfort to truly reconnect.

That impulse—to provide, to cover the costs, to make sure no one goes without—has been with me my whole life. Even as a kid, I carried a tiny blue Hello Kitty wallet, though I wasn't even ten. It never left my side. Inside were two things: a scrap of paper filled with corny jokes to lift my mood on the worst days, and another with a list of ten people who called me "little Dolores." That list reminded me of who I was to others, even when I felt weighed down by responsibilities that made me feel far older than my years. I never got the chance to be a carefree child, so I learned early to take care of others—and to find small, secret ways to take care of myself too.

My middle sister made it clear that she was not interested in spending time with me. My younger sister was open to the trip. Paying for the trip to Switzerland felt good —like a gift to myself, though it was really for all of us. I imagined long afternoons with my little sister, walking through the streets, laughing over coffee, and finally having the kind of conversations we had been avoiding for years. I thought the lightness of vacation would make the heavier things easier to carry.

But travel, like family, can be unpredictable. I've always believed that taking care of the logistics—paying for the plane tickets, covering hotel rooms, even buying Emilio's endless sneaker collection—would somehow take care of the deeper issues too. If everyone's needs were met, then maybe I could finally turn to my own.

It has never worked that way. Instead, I kept running myself into the ground, caught in a cycle of caretaking that left me depleted and resentful. Sometimes, in my scramble to help, I ended up abandoning the very people who needed me most—like my youngest sister.

The one thing I was most excited for on my birthday trip was to take my nephew and niece to the karaoke ski gondola. It was one of those enclosed, round gondolas set on rails, with a small stage at the front, speakers, and a microphone dangling from above. You could stand or sit on the benches lining the sides, but there wasn't much room. Sofia, my niece and nephew, and I squeezed onto the first gondola. We sat right down while the kids fought for their seats. They wiggled and fidgeted the whole ride, pointing at the passing scenery. In the hubbub, my youngest sister and her husband ended up on a different gondola. They had gone back to grab some extra tickets we forgot.

I was thrilled my sister had decided to join us on the trip. My first attempt at calling her to make amends hadn't gone that well. We talked but didn't get very deep. The barriers between us had been up too long and couldn't be lowered so easily. I had hoped the trip would be our chance to come together, away from daily distractions, in a place that was neutral and fun.

The gondola ride was awesome. We sang, laughed, and tried to keep the younger kids from slipping off the benches or leaning too far over the railing. When we got back to the base, everyone was smiling, joking, and waiting for my sister's gondola to arrive. When her gondola finally steadied, she stormed out and threw bags, skis, poles, and helmets on the floor.

"This is the second time today that you do this to me!" she screamed, followed by a string of other unexpected grievances.

I was shocked. All of this over riding in a different

gondola? It was like watching our dad explode over nothing again.

"Number one, do not yell at me," I told her, "and number two, you are acting like Dad."

That might not have been the best choice of words. She continued screaming, ending by saying it was psychological warfare to compare her to our dad.

"Can you please stop yelling?" I asked her.

"I am not yelling," she yelled while everyone else turned to look at us. "My volume is just high."

I didn't acknowledge how contradictory her statement was. I simply wanted to return to quiet. "Look," I told her, focusing on keeping my voice at a reasonable volume, "I'm over fifty now. I don't react well when people yell at me. I can't tolerate it now. I'm allergic. Besides, it's my birthday."

Once my sister was done with her gondola tantrum and walked away, I looked at Sofia. "Wasn't that terrible? She overreacts for nothing," I said.

"Well," she responded, looking at me thoughtfully, "you were exactly the same way before you started your treatment."

I felt awful. I never realized I had ever been that bad, that quick to react and scream. But once Sofia called it out, memories came rushing back—countless times I had yelled over small things. Whether it was Emilio letting the cat escape or a car cutting me off in traffic, I did yell—a lot. And I hadn't fully confronted it. Even after therapy and learning so much, I was still discovering elements of my own behavior I hadn't understood, or even seen, at the time. I apologized to Sofia.

Growing up, explosive emotions were the normal baseline for my family. From my mother's chaos, swinging from tears to hysterical laughter, to my father's misplaced anger, everyone just shouted their feelings when we were children. That was how we learned to express ourselves—or at least how we learned to survive emotionally.

For years, I had assumed my youngest sister had been spared from all of it. She didn't get to experience the worst. Watching her unravel on the gondola, however, made it clear she hadn't escaped unscathed. The patterns were there—the snap, the intensity, the inability to pause. Just like I could now see some of my parents' bad behavior in myself, I could see it in her too.

I could tell she was stressed. It's possible that it was her kid that really set her off during the trip. She had managed our fucked-up childhood reasonably well, masking the lingering tension, but now, with a young hyperactive child, everything became amplified for her, bringing the stress to the forefront. It was hard to watch her try to calm him and to keep him out of trouble while her own emotions simmered just beneath the surface. She was like a ticking time bomb—raw feelings layered over exhaustion, over responsibility, and over our inherited habits. Anything could set her off, and it often did. It was heartbreaking but also revealing, a reminder that some cycles repeat until they are consciously noticed and addressed.

When I suggested that my nephew might need treatment, she didn't take it well.

On the walk back to the hotel, Sofia and I talked more about my sister and nephew. She had noticed yet another recurring theme that I had completely missed. I was still pissed off, thinking my sister had ruined my birthday over a gondola ride—but Sofia pointed out that it was way bigger than that. I had taken a different gondola than my sister twice that day. I was used to being independent, so I thought nothing of it. I would have enjoyed the ride regardless. If it had been me on the second gondola. I wouldn't have thought twice about it.

Sofia, however, saw the thread running through all of it. She explained calmly, with the kind of clarity I sometimes lacked when I was too close to the emotions, that she could see my sister hadn't let go of me leaving her decades ago—first to do my social service in the jungle and later to move to the United States. That abandonment wasn't buried under time for her; it was just below the surface, in her memory and in her unconscious mind. The wound was refreshed and reopened by the slightest touch.

Even if the gondola fiasco hadn't happened, Sofia said, my sister was going to blow up during the trip. The ride had simply become a trigger, a surface-level spark for a deeper, long-held frustration. She had pent-up emotions that needed release, and no amount of vacation planning or fun activities could erase that. Sofia's perspective made me realize how blind I had been to my sister's internal world, seeing only the explosion without recognizing the pressure building for years. I had managed to leave her once again, this time by taking a different gondola.

A few hours later, we all went out for dinner. My sister acted like nothing had happened. She was chipper and kind, as if the earlier explosion had never occurred. It was the same pattern my dad had followed for years. He would scream, break things, beat everyone up, and then act like it was all behind him, inviting us to go out and enjoy ourselves. The contradiction was jarring, disorienting, and exhausting.

I remembered the day I threatened to kill my dad with a knife. My dad had just finished beating my mother and screaming at my middle sister. They were battered, bruised, and crying. I didn't know how to comfort them, but at least threatening him made him leave for a short while. Half an hour later, he came back, asking if we wanted to go have a picnic in the countryside. It was insane.

Watching my sister follow the same pattern was unsettling.

"Why are you so quiet?" she asked me.

I just stared at her. I wanted the meal to end, to retreat to my room, and to process the day in private. All the kids had witnessed her outburst. Seeing her pattern mirrored my father's—the yelling, the sudden calm, the pretense that nothing had happened—was disheartening, and I couldn't help but wonder if my niece and nephew would turn out the same way. It reminded me of how deeply these cycles run and how painful it is to watch them repeat in the next generation. The day's events left me drained.

I probably won't plan another family birthday trip. Until very recently, I did not celebrate my birthday. My birthday was just a regular day. Nothing special about it. I didn't want the spotlight. Plus, I didn't want to celebrate getting older. From my history of brushes with death and being surrounded by violence and illness, any reminder of my aging always felt like another step toward the grave.

That said, I was grateful for the chance to be active in Switzerland. Between my hip, my back, and now my knee, it was the most movement I'd had in a while. After years of working out with soldiers or hobbling around on crutches, it felt like an enjoyable middle ground—challenging but possible. I could keep up with my niece and nephew, explore new places, and feel capable in a way I hadn't in years.

After therapy, I decided to celebrate my birthday as a way of being thankful to be alive. Embracing my birthday and aging has become a new way for me to celebrate life. It's symbolic of a healthy change—I have a new way of doing things where I don't let the fear of aging and death dictate my life. It's opened me up to more optimistic expectations.

Overall, my nephews seemed to really enjoy the Switzerland trip, and I appreciated the brief escape it gave all of us. Even with the chaos and outbursts, there were moments of laughter and connection that reminded me why family—imperfect and complicated—is worth showing up for, even if only for a short while. Watching my sister and niece and nephew navigate their own frustrations, I couldn't help but notice the patterns repeating—the echoes of my parents' emotional intensity and all the inherited ways we learned to react under stress. And yet, by witnessing them consciously, I also recognized my own choices within those patterns: when to step back, when to care, and when to finally take care of myself. The trip, messy and exhausting as it was, became another important lesson in understanding the limits of what I can control.

I couldn't control how our childhood affected my sisters, but I spent years trying to control every detail to avoid bad surprises. My default was to control all variables, including my sisters, and they now resent me for it. Any suggestion that I make to them nowadays triggers an immediate rejection from them. They feel like I am trying to control them yet again.

My middle sister has been living in Germany for some time now. She has two children, and the trauma of our childhood affected her life just as deeply as it did mine. It shows in the way she takes care of her children. She defines herself as the perfect mother. She's determined to be flawless and to protect her kids from every possible harm. They live in Berlin, but she raises them as if they were cut off from the world.

One year, I asked her what the small kids wanted for

presents. "Do they like toys? Maybe slime or water guns?" I suggested.

She cut me off immediately. "Absolutely not. No toys. Just books."

Perhaps this is her own version of the game of silence.

Just like I tried to control all the elements of my life, she tries to control everything about her kids' lives. Our parents hadn't been able to protect us, and now she spends her life building walls of safety around her children.

In some ways, she might have had it the hardest of us all. She was born just two years after Javiercito died. No one can replace a dead child, but in some ways, she was forced into that role before she could even form memories.

Our lives have been defined by movement as well. Just like me, my sisters have lived in a string of different places: my youngest sister in Spain, our middle sister in Germany, and even Sofia in multiple countries. None of us stayed in Colombia; none of us stayed still. It's in our genes, a legacy of fleeing, of survival, of seeking new spaces. Even if we aren't running from violence like my grandfather escaping the Nazis, the rhythm of travel, the habit of packing up, the limbo of moving, navigating transport, and adjusting to new places is embedded in us. Bogotá, Tres Esquinas, New York, New England, Florida, Scotland, London, France—moving, adapting, and finding our footing is just what we do. *Pate perro* for life.

All of us were saddened by losing Javiercito. A few years ago, I was searching for a document in my attic when I stumbled across a poem I had written after he died. It was tucked away in a binder, below heaps of paperwork that had been building up for years. I didn't remember writing the poem, but I recognized it; the feelings were familiar. It brought me back to watching model airplanes fly over his grave, flailing my little arms in the sky, trying to catch the planes. Some of those memories are vivid. The house lit up on the day he died, my ruby red shoes, visiting his gravesite, his chubby face, the whir of plane engines—those moments all stayed with me. I must have been around five years old when I wrote the poem. A reminder that children are affected by trauma and loss.

Awareness and insight have allowed me to observe and understand my emotions and the patterns in myself and in my family. Acknowledging them has given me a sense of agency I didn't have as a child. I am no longer entirely at the mercy of repeated cycles. I can choose when to step back, when to engage, when to care for others, and when to finally care for myself. By understanding my family's chaos, our escapes, and our movements, I was able to care for my scars. Those experiences have also taught me adaptability and resilience. The future is uncertain, of course, but I keep going. Carrying both the lessons and the successes from my past, I am ready to create moments that reflect my love of planes and travel, while also venturing to calmer environments. I am ready to create the next chapter that is finally, fully my own.

JAVIERCITO

WHEN HE WAS BORN, *he ate a lot.*
Javiercito sat in his highchair
Javiercito would look out from his crib.
He would look at the children.
Javiercito was blond.
He slept like a little frog.
He was so cute and pure.
He was so noble.
My mom loved him a lot.
My dad did as well.
I adored him.
He rides his pony rocker.
He rides his swing.
He holds his bottle and would play with his belly button.
Javiercito looks at the Christmas tree.
There was a sheep, and he would play with it all the time.
Sitting in the living room playing with the green car.
Tucked in his crib.

He loves yellow eggs.
The little planes fly over the flowers we take to Javiercito.

" *Individuals who believe they are masters of their fate are as a rule the slaves of destiny.*"

CARL JUNG

Dolores Furtch grew up in Colombia where she received her MD degree. She specialized as a psychiatrist in the US and has worked in the field for over 20 years. After finally integrating the pain from her past, Dolores is determined to get new scars but this time only while on skis.